T0285938

Snorkelling Adventures
around Vancouver Island
and the Gulf Islands

SNORKELLING ADVENTURES AROUND VANCOUVER ISLAND AND THE GULF ISLANDS

The Ultimate Guide

SARA ELLISON

HARBOUR PUBLISHING

Copyright © 2023 Sara Ellison
2 3 4 5 6 — 27 26 25 24 23

All rights reserved. No part of this publication may be reproduced, stored in a retrieval system or transmitted, in any form or by any means, without prior permission of the publisher or, in the case of photocopying or other reprographic copying, a licence from Access Copyright, www.accesscopyright.ca, 1-800-893-5777, info@accesscopyright.ca.

Harbour Publishing Co. Ltd.
P.O. Box 219, Madeira Park, BC, V0N 2H0
www.harbourpublishing.com

All photographs by the author except where noted
Edited by Brian Lynch
Indexed by Chandan Kumar Singh
Cover and text design by Libris Simas Ferraz/Onça Publishing
Printed and bound in South Korea

Harbour Publishing acknowledges the support of the Canada Council for the Arts, the Government of Canada, and the Province of British Columbia through the BC Arts Council.

This guidebook is intended for informational purposes only. Neither the author nor the publisher can accept liability for any loss or injury incurred by anyone using this book.

Library and Archives Canada Cataloguing in Publication

Title: Snorkelling adventures around Vancouver Island and the Gulf Islands : the ultimate guide / Sara Ellison.
Names: Ellison, Sara, author.
Description: Includes bibliographical references and index.
Identifiers: Canadiana (print) 20220458324 | Canadiana (ebook) 20220458960 | ISBN 9781990776151 (softcover) | ISBN 9781990776168 (ebook)
Subjects: LCSH: Skin diving—British Columbia—Vancouver Island—Guidebooks. | LCSH: Skin diving—British Columbia—Gulf Islands—Guidebooks. | LCSH: Vancouver Island (B.C.)—Guidebooks. | LCSH: Gulf Islands (B.C.)—Guidebooks. | LCGFT: Guidebooks.
Classification: LCC GV838.673.C3 E45 2023 | DDC 797.2/32097112—dc23

The author at the short plumose
anemone–covered Royston wrecks.
Photo by Jon Willis

Ochre stars and giant plumose anemones.

CONTENTS

Greater Victoria

The West Coast

The Gulf Islands

Cowichan to Comox

The North Island (Campbell River and Beyond)

Orange peel nudibranch.

SNORKELLING AROUND VANCOUVER ISLAND... SERIOUSLY?

The chilly waters of coastal British Columbia might not be at the top of most people's snorkel destination lists. Indeed, even local ocean enthusiasts, gung-ho when it comes to kayaking and paddleboarding, are more likely to think about heading to Hawaii or the Caribbean when it comes to actually submerging their bodies *in* the water, rather than cruising on its surface. But BC has long been known as a premier scuba diving location. We may not have the expansive coral reefs or eye-popping fish species of more tropical destinations, but the underwater world of the Pacific Northwest is both colourful and biodiverse. Here, you can commune with the giant Pacific octopus and face-off with curmudgeonly wolf-eels who hang out in predictable locations like Grandpa on his porch. Cold-water coral species, sponges and tunicates draw from a palette every bit as vivid as their tropical cousins. The fish are surprisingly diverse, ranging from the impossibly cute, inch-long Pacific spiny lumpsucker to the mammoth lingcod and fantastically colourful greenling species. Finally, the invertebrate life—with over 25 species of sea stars, spectacular anemones and the sheer eye candy of the nudibranch family—is simply world-class. No wonder that scuba diving has an avid and numerous following around Vancouver Island—the ocean's delights are right here on our doorstep, without the need

Giant plumose anemones in Kuldekduma Channel.

for spending thousands of dollars, weeks of vacation time and tonnes of CO_2 to get there.

Despite the wonders of scuba diving, this is not a wholly accessible hobby. Finances are perhaps the most obvious significant barrier. An introductory scuba course will likely set you back to the tune of $700 or so (depending on where you do it). Much more significant is the investment in gear, which becomes particularly pricey for cold-water locations thanks to the requirement for a dry suit, which can quickly approach price tags in the thousands of dollars. A second factor that puts many people off the scuba route is the hassle of dealing with all the bulky equipment. Tanks are heavy, and lugging them to and from the dive site can be physically demanding. For example, the Ogden Point Breakwater, one of Victoria's most popular dive locations, requires hauling your gear almost a kilometre from the car and then negotiating metre-high concrete blocks to descend to the water level. Any significant swell only adds to the drama, as water ingress and egress quickly deteriorates into a washing machine experience that leaves you feeling pounded and exhausted (and with a newfound admiration for seals). And, of course, even if you have your own tanks, you still have to pay for, and factor in the logistical overhead of, refilling them before each dive.

Snorkelling is eminently more accessible than scuba diving to the average ocean-lover, in terms of both financial investment and hassle factor. Yet, despite this apparently obvious combination of wonderful ocean offerings and an accessible activity, snorkelling in BC has few resources available to those wanting to get started. This lack of advice might seem unimportant—what could be simpler than just strapping on a mask and jumping in? Indeed, many of you have probably done exactly that on your tropical vacations, without the need for any particular pointers or guidance. Well, this is not Hawaii, my friends. I don't need to tell you that jumping in at your local beach in your bathing suit is just not going to cut it. In addition to the

Opalescent (long-horned) nudibranch.

almost instant hypothermia, the currents along our shores can be vicious, and the intertidal wildlife not always obvious. Having some local intel is essential to staying warm and safe, as well as to knowing just where (and when) to go to see the interesting critters. All of this is necessary for an enjoyable and rewarding snorkel experience.

In this book, I will explain all the gear you need to stay warm and safe while snorkelling, describe in detail the access and tips to destinations around the island, and even provide some photos to help get you started on species identification. You're going to love it. And loving the ocean has two important outcomes. First, I hope that it will simply bring you as much joy as it brings me, and that snorkelling will offer a peaceful and fulfilling distraction to your busy lives. Second, and arguably more importantly, I hope that the wonder that you discover under the waves will lead to a better understanding of the Pacific Ocean's value as an ecosystem. The world's oceans, and their myriad inhabitants, are fragile and in peril. Experiencing the Pacific's treasures first-hand is the very best way to appreciate what we have to lose, whether it be by overfishing, pipeline development or pollution. By spreading the gospel of snorkelling, you will be advocating for the future health of one of the most important ecosystems on our planet.

ABOUT THIS GUIDE
(Some Notes, Caveats and Cautions)

The main body of this book is a destination guide. For each location, I have provided a brief description of the shoreline in terms of terrain and access. Most of the places described in this guide are well established, and the access is unlikely to change much. However, the world is always on the move: parking restrictions change (or are introduced), signage gets moved and remote locations get developed. None of this is my fault, and I take no responsibility for any inaccuracy of the on-the-ground information in this book due to change that has occurred since the time of writing!

Although most of the locations in this guide are road/trail accessible, some require boat access. The added adventure of cruising to your snorkel destination, as well as the seclusion that normally accompanies the extra effort, can make these boat access destinations particularly memorable excursions. For some of the boat access destinations in this guide, the water crossings are short, and can be achieved by kayak, canoe or paddleboard. In other locations, more challenging water conditions or sheer distance require a motorized craft. Such destinations are definitely more exclusive, but I have included them here for those of you lucky enough to have a boat (or, even better, a friend with a boat). Indeed, if you plan to snorkel around the North Island, there are relatively few shore-based locations, due to the lack of road infrastructure outside the main towns.

The giant Pacific octopus can be found in as little as a metre of water.

With each destination entry, I have provided a list of species that I have personally seen at that location. This list is biased and incomplete, reflecting the creatures that I have found notable at a particular spot. For example, I readily admit to being far more interested in invertebrate life than in fish, and as a result of my piscine apathy, I am not very good at identifying the latter. I therefore rarely include extensive fish species in my critter lists, unless I have seen something particularly noteworthy. I am also less-than-expert on things with shells; from clams to crabs and chitons, most molluscs and crustaceans get short shrift on my species list. On the other hand, I'm pretty darn keen on nudibranchs, sea stars and anemones. In short, my critter lists should be considered only as a guide, and you will surely find many more species in any given place than I have recorded here.

It should also be emphasized that, while encounters with marine mammals can happen inadvertently, when humans get too close to wild animals in their habitat we risk causing stress and disturbing them. Coming face-to-mask with a sea lion causes my own blood pressure to rise too. It is both the law and common sense to keep your distance from seals, sea lions and cetaceans for the safety and well-being of all involved. For the most current federal laws and regulations on watching marine life, visit the Canadian Department of Fisheries and Oceans website (www.dfo -mpo.gc.ca).

Snorkelling is primarily a surface activity. However, my critter lists include species that I have seen in approximately the top 10 metres of the water column, for several reasons. First, the tides around Vancouver Island are highly variable, changing by up to 5 metres through the days and months in some locations. The intertidal habitat is therefore huge, and what you can see from the surface on one day requires diving down 5 metres on another. Second, although beginner snorkellers will be content with poking around at the surface, as you get more experienced, confident and curious, you are probably going to start diving down. At first, these duck dives will be just a metre or two, but in time you may get comfortable going farther (at which point you should consider taking a freediving course). However, in practice, the vast majority of the species listed in this book are found in the top 5 metres, so there is no need for any kind of underwater critter FOMO. Finally, 10 metres is the visibility you can hope for on a good day, such that with optimal conditions and a sharp pair of eyes, even the surface snorkeller can glimpse into the shallow subtidal zone.

In addition to my critter list for every entry in this guide, for some destinations I have also included a description of "signature species" that are particularly noteworthy for that specific location. In some cases, the signature species may be a creature that

A typical West Coast scene: ochre sea stars and green surf anemones.

is not commonly found around the islands but is readily found at that spot. For example, the critically endangered sunflower star is quite common at East Sooke Park's Aylard Farm, strawberry anemones (usually only a sight for scuba divers) can be found at snorkel depths at Possession Point, and I have only ever seen bat stars at Ucluelet locations. In other cases, the signature species designation indicates the sheer abundance of a certain critter, such as the plumose anemone colonies at Argonaut Wharf and Echo Bay. However, bear in mind that while anemones are static and hence their presence as a signature species is reliable, most animals are mobile, which means their observation can never be guaranteed.

I have illustrated this guide with my own photographs, both to inspire and to serve as an aid to species identification. I encourage you to flip through the entire book to familiarize yourself with some of our local species, so that you will have some knowledge when you venture out underwater. However, not only are the photos in this book an incomplete sampling of BC's intertidal life, but they are also not organized by species (rather, they are ordered to complement the destination guide and narrative of the text), nor do I provide any details on taxonomy. Indeed, this book is not intended to be a species reference, and I encourage you to invest in one of the excellent field guides that specifically aspire to this purpose.

Your experience at a given snorkel site will depend on a number of factors, including conditions on the day, as well as the particular aspects of the activity that you find rewarding. Even a great location can feel underwhelming if the visibility is poor, the critters all seem to be hiding, the swell is churning, or if you're simply having a bad day (leaky mask, cold hands or any number of the technical challenges that come with cold-water snorkelling). With those caveats in mind, I have awarded a star rating to my personal favourite locations in each chapter. While all of the destinations in this book are worth a visit, the starred locations consistently reward the snorkeller with some of the best wildlife offerings in the region. Nonetheless, the West Coast and North Island chapters are somewhat more star-heavy than the others, reflecting the fact that these parts of Vancouver Island's coastline host some of the most spectacular cold water bounty in the world.

SAFETY

Snorkelling is not an inherently dangerous sport. Unlike scuba diving, you'll be spending most of your time at the surface and likely not more than a few tens of metres offshore. Nonetheless, any ocean-based activity carries with it some potential hazards. Safety and risk awareness are everyone's personal responsibility. A complete treatise on snorkelling safety is beyond the scope of this guide, but here are some of the primary factors for which you should be prepared.

Since wildlife relies on its food bounty being delivered on the conveyor belt of the ocean's daily change, much of the best critter spotting is to be had in areas that experience strong currents. It is recommended to check the current tables for your intended destination before each outing. Wind and waves are also a factor, although snorkelling in choppy seas is more likely to be unpleasant rather than dangerous. Always assess conditions before you enter the water, and regularly check that you are still able to swim back the way you came.

Boat traffic usually doesn't come close enough to shore to be a risk for snorkellers, but be vigilant particularly around marinas, recreational areas and popular fishing spots. Any offshore crossings should be made in a group, preferably with a flag or buoy to enhance visibility.

Getting snagged on fishing line is a potential hazard in both urban and recreational areas. Always swim with a dive knife and practise deploying it while underwater (so that if you ever need it, you instinctively know where it is). Getting tangled in kelp is a common fear for beginner snorkellers, but in practice this is

Fried egg jellies may look intimidating, but their sting is mild.

very unlikely, as it's usually easy to tug free even in the thickest of forests.

There is little to fear from marine life in our island's waters. There is nothing man-eating or deadly venomous. The most unpleasant sting you might receive is from the lion's mane jelly (but almost all the other jelly species are harmless). Your other main risk of an underwater owie is from a close call with a sea urchin. These critters come in three colour varieties: green, red (which are sometimes, confusingly, purple) and purple, and their

Green, purple and red urchins.

spines will easily penetrate neoprene if handled incorrectly. Once you know how to handle them, though, harvesting is encouraged—the decline of some of their natural predators (such as sunflower stars and otters) is leading to infestations of ravenous urchins destroying many coastal kelp forests.

The final creature caveat I will offer is regarding sea lions. These beasts can be huge and territorial. Unlike harbour seals, which are curious but ultimately skittish, sea lions can be boisterous and confident. Extended interactions tend to embolden them further. While they are unlikely to do you any serious harm, I find close brushes with sea lions unnerving, and retreat before they start nipping at my fins and fingers.

If your snorkelling adventures lure you toward diving beyond the top few metres, a freediving course will equip you with the physiological and safety knowledge pertinent to pushing your depths and your lungs. A freediving course will also help you calibrate your weight belt requirements—being overweighted is a major safety no-no regardless of your depth destination.

Snorkel safely out there—dive with a buddy, check conditions before you go, and get out before you feel cold or tired.

GEAR

Wetsuits

Before answering the question "What type of wetsuit do I need?" it is important to appreciate that the water temperatures around Vancouver Island are highly variable, both with location and season. The West Coast is exposed to the open ocean, and even in the summertime the coastal water has little opportunity to stockpile any significant warmth. The same is true for the northern and southern parts of the island, which experience daily flushing by the tides. Seasonal water temperatures around Victoria, for example, typically range from 8 to 12°C , so it is fairly chilly even in the height of summer. On the other hand, the central east coast experiences much less replacement from the open ocean and is consequently able to accrue some of the sun's energy. The waters between Duncan and Campbell River can get almost tropical (well, by Canadian standards) in the summertime, reaching temperatures of 18°C or more. The same is true of protected bays around the island, including the Saanich Inlet.

If you plan to be a summer-only snorkeller and restrict yourself to the warmer waters around Vancouver Island, you will likely be able to get by in a modest-thickness wetsuit—an off-the-shelf 5mm wetsuit will likely do you just fine. But for those snorkellers who would like to explore the wider extent of Vancouver Island's coastline, or snorkel beyond the summer months, additional wetsuit guidance is required.

Wetsuits come in two basic flavours: open cell and closed cell. The distinction is whether or not the raw neoprene rubber is lined with a fabric (usually polyester) to make it more resistant to damage, such as nicks and tears. The presence of a fabric lining is referred to as closed cell, whereas bare neoprene on your skin is called open cell. While the fabric lining makes closed cell much tougher than open cell, the resilience comes at the cost of warmth. With bare open cell neoprene against your skin, the tiny bubbles in the rubber form a seal with your body. It is usually considered that open cell neoprene is worth an extra 2mm in thickness compared with closed cell. For example, a 3mm open cell wetsuit provides the same insulation as a 5mm closed cell. You'll be able to find open cell wetsuits in a variety of thicknesses. If you are snorkelling anywhere outside the east-central coast in the summertime, you'll want an open cell suit of either 5mm or 7mm thickness in order to be ready for temperatures in the low teens (and below). Such suits are often marketed for either free-diving or spearfishing.

Two other design features will equip you with maximal warmth. First, make sure your suit has an integrated hood; a separate hood, even well tucked in, offers the ocean one more possible ingress to your body around the gap at the neck. Second, choose a two-piece suit (Farmer John/Jane plus jacket), which provides you with a double layer of coverage over your core.

Hands and Feet

Having your body insulated is most of the battle, but you'll get sad pretty quickly if your feet and hands are not covered. For hands, a standard pair of 5mm diving gloves is what most people use. Make sure to tuck them up inside your wetsuit sleeve to minimize water ingress.

There are a few possible options for footwear. Option one is boot style—these often have a thick rubber sole and side zip. The terrific advantage of a dive boot is that you can walk in them over sharp rocks and barnacles with nary a second thought to any damage. If you're facing one of BC's typically rocky water entries, or if you're doing a drift snorkel that requires you to hike back to your starting point, this is a very handy feature. There are two main downsides to a hard-soled dive boot. First, the presence of a zipper allows water to leak in very quickly; wearing a thick wool sock underneath helps considerably with warmth, even when wet. The second is that the stiff, thick sole will only fit into fins with an adjustable foot pocket. If you have (or want to have) fancy freediving fins, or indeed anything with a soft rubber foot pocket, the boot style will not provide a snug fit.

The alternative is a neoprene sock, which you will likely want in a 5mm thickness for BC waters (7mm in both socks and gloves is hard to find, and 5mm actually does the job pretty well). Although some socks have light reinforcement on the soles, in general they are simple closed cell neoprene all over. If worn well-tucked into your wetsuit, the lack of a zip or seam means that there should be minimal water entry and your tootsies will likely stay a lot warmer than in a boot with a zip. However, you'll not be hiking over any barnacle-covered terrain.

Weight Belts

Now you are all layered up and ready to go! Well, maybe not quite. All that neoprene will make you incredibly buoyant. This is no bad thing if you are planning to stay on the surface, or if you are a beginner and want to feel very safe and floaty. However, many snorkellers like to duck dive down a few (or more) metres to take a closer look at the critters or explore the shallow subtidal zone. You will find it completely impossible (but highly amusing) to try to duck dive when you are under layers of cushy open cell neoprene unless you have a weight belt. This is a common accessory in scuba (and free) diving and easy to pick up at any dive store.

While there exist some online calculators that claim to be able to predict how much lead weight you will need, the reality is that everyone's body has a different intrinsic buoyancy (which can change over time), and that buoyancy also depends on your wetsuit. The only way to know how much weight you need is to try it out. A good dive shop will let you buy your weights and return any that you find you don't need—but check the return policy before you buy.

A calibration technique that works well for snorkellers (and is also espoused in the freediving community as a good rule of thumb to get you started) is to have enough weight on your belt that when you are vertical in the water and do a normal (not full/aggressive) exhale, your nose and mouth are still above the waterline. The reasoning here is obvious: if you find yourself in trouble, you want to have both of your airways above the waterline. In practice, calibrating this weight means spending some time at the beach with a stack of weights and gradually putting pounds on a little at a time until you find this balance point. Purchasing a selection of lead denominations is very helpful, so that you can both balance the number of items on your belt (a string of 10 one-pound weights is a tad cumbersome, but a single 10-pounder will feel equally uncomfortable) and fine-tune things in the margins. I cannot emphasize enough that overweighting can be a dangerous business. While you might be tempted to pile on a few extra pounds to help your duck dive, you never want to be having to fight to get back to the surface. Take your approach to weight calibration conservatively—lead is modular and easy to add if you need more, so there is no harm in taking a season to slowly add a little at a time until you find the safe sweet spot that is right for you.

Fins

Many people will begin their snorkelling career without fins—I happily pootled around in just a pair of booties for years. However, having a basic pair of fins will not set you back very much in the pocket-money department and offers several advantages.

First, safety. If you are snorkelling anywhere with a chance of significant current (and that is many of the places in this book!), having the ability to get yourself safely back to shore (and your car keys) is essential. Second, if you want to cover any significant distance, say from shore to a nearby islet, you are going to be *very* slow if you don't have fins. Finally, there will likely come a time when you are no longer satisfied with surface views. Maybe you have glimpsed something just beyond your vision that you desperately want to give a closer look. Maybe your buddy surfaces to report a giant Pacific octopus hanging out a few metres down. Or perhaps you just want to explore a little farther into the shallow subtidal zone in search of orange sea pens. Fins are your engine to achieve those slightly deeper excursions.

Fins come in a variety of lengths and materials. The entry-level option (which is perfectly good for pretty much every occasion) is a pair of plastic scuba fins. If you would like to progress to a more powerful option (or simply indulge your inner mermaid fetish), freediving fins have much longer blades and will make duck diving an easier endeavour. Freediving fins can be plastic, fibreglass or carbon fibre (in order of both price and performance). Plastic is the most hard-wearing of these materials but is also heavy. Carbon fibre is more easily scratched and damaged but is lightweight and high-performance.

Accessories and Optional Extras

Do yourself a favour and ask Santa for a dive knife. These are fairly cheap to buy, and while you will likely never have to use it, it is an essential part of your safety set-up. Getting snagged on fishing line is the most common concern, but a knife covers a host of eventualities.

A large plastic tote box is a very handy multi-purpose accessory. You can use it to transport all your dry gear from your house to the car; you can chuck all your wet gear back in it once you are done; and then you can easily carry it back inside (or to the garden) and fill it with fresh water for your swill and cleanup.

You may also wish to bring a yoga mat—no, not to celebrate your communing with nature with a few sun salutations, but to give your cold, bare feet something clean and soft to stand on while you're changing. No more awkward, one-legged balancing on your sandals while trying to stay off the dirt of the parking lot! You don't even need a full mat; I slice about two feet of length off with a box cutter, which provides just enough change space without taking up too much room in my gear box.

Commonly used by freedivers and scuba divers, a buoy is another accessory to consider for your collection if you will be more than a few metres away from the shore. A buoy not only maximizes your visibility to boat traffic, but also gives you a float to hang on to if you're feeling in need of rest. Many buoys also have a handy storage section in the centre, giving you a place to stuff the sandals that you wore down to the beach, snacks, drinks, this guidebook and any other accessory you can't do without.

Underwater photography adds a new dimension to your snorkelling escapades. Indeed, some of BC's Pacific critters are small enough that they may escape your attention while you are in the water, and it is only when browsing your photos on the big screen that you can fully appreciate all that you have captured. A camera is also extremely useful for species identification. You may well think that that bright yellow nudibranch will be easy-peasy to pick out in your field guide from the comfort of your couch, but I guarantee that beginners, at least, will be left pondering the details of the tubercles and branchial plumes in order to distinguish your Monterey from your noble sea lemon. A camera is the best choice for stills and close-ups, whereas a GoPro is better for video.

There are many camera and GoPro options on the market that are waterproof to 15 metres or so without a housing. Nonetheless, a housing is a good idea for protecting your gadget from bumps and scratches, and will extend its lifetime. (Even with careful rinsing after each use, the seals will eventually be degraded by the salt.) Final photography pearl of wisdom: get a wrist strap. It sounds so obvious, but simply holding your camera while you swim is a recipe for Lost Camera Sadness.

BEST DESTINATIONS FOR...

Some folks are in it for the adventure, some for the therapy of the ocean's embrace, some for the wildlife photography, and others for pushing their depth limits. Whether you are looking for a place that will appeal to family members left on dry land, remote boat-only access, or a particular species that you are hankering after, the destinations in this guide offer something for everyone. Here are my personal top picks to satisfy your every watery whim.

Sea Stars

With over 25 species of sea stars in the Pacific Northwest, there are so many multi-armed wonders to discover, and the majority can be found at snorkel-friendly depths. From the giant (but now critically endangered) sunflower star and the many colour variations of the striped sunstar to the adorably pudgy cushion star, I never tire of these diverse denizens of the Asteroidea class (such a fitting astronomical moniker for these marine stars!).

- **Aylard Farm** (East Sooke Park) is one of the most reliable South Island locations to find sunflower stars, a species that has been placed on the critically endangered list as a result of the sea star wasting disease that hit the extended Pacific coast from 2013 to 2016.
- **Iron Mine Bay** (also at East Sooke Park) has one of the best varieties of sea stars anywhere on Vancouver Island. Striped sunstars, northern sunstars and rainbow stars are all frequently seen, and I have spotted several of the less

Striped sunstars come in a variety of colours, but with a central stripe that is almost always blue.

common (for snorkellers) species here as well, such as the spiny red star, velcro star, cushion star and giant pink star.

- **Plumper Wall** in the North Island is one of the rare spots where snorkellers can see basket stars. For the taxon pedant, I will note that basket stars are technically brittle stars (class Ophiuroidea), which are distinct from sea stars (class Asteroidea).

- **Ogden Point Breakwater** is one of the best in-Victoria spots for sea stars. In addition to hosting the more common species, such as leather stars, ochre stars and blood stars, it's a great place for vermilion stars, cushion stars and striped sunstars.
- **Terrace Beach** (Ucluelet) offers abundant bat stars, which I've seen only along this part of the coastline, as well as plenty of large and colourful mottled stars.

Nudibranchs

Nudibranchs are the darlings of the underwater photographer and one of the favourite critter families among snorkellers in general. I tend to have the best luck spotting nudis in the early fall, often in locations that have been hiding under weeds all summer but are now exposed as the vegetation dies back. Sea slugs in the intertidal zone seem to prefer more protected locations, and I find them much less commonly in high-current areas.

- **Telegraph Cove** is a great little Victoria spot for nudibranchs, and tends to be sheltered from prevailing winds and strong currents. Follow the shoreline from the left of the beach and move slowly to inspect all the rocky real estate.
- **Clover Point** is one of my favourite in-Victoria locations, and is home to more Monterey nudibranchs than you can shake a stick at, as well as abundant clown, leopard and frosted varieties. You also stand a good chance of finding noble sea lemons.
- The **Gillingham Islands** (Greater Victoria) are a joy for the nudibranch lover, particularly the channel that runs between the two main islands. On a good day you will come away with at least half a dozen species under your belt. If you don't find clowns here, then you are simply not looking.
- **Peter Cove** on Pender Island is prime nudibranch stomping ground. It's best to come here in the fall; not only are the

Red-gilled nudibranch.

rock walls free of vegetation, but boats have been packed away for the winter, leaving docks and mooring buoys open for exploration.

- The twin coves of **Terrace Beach** and **Little Beach** in Ucluelet are replete with a variety of nudibranchs. Large noble sea lemons are abundant, and you have a good chance of spotting San Diego dorids—the heavyweight cousin of the more commonly found leopard dorid.
- Late September/early October is party time for hooded nudibranchs. Any location with a rich kelp patch or eelgrass beds merits close inspection as the water temperatures start their decline back toward single digits. **Ogden Point**

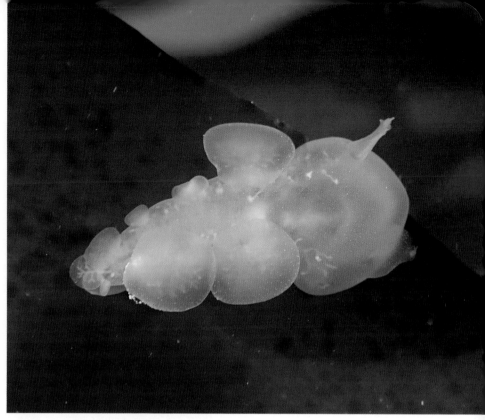

Hooded nudibranch resting on a kelp frond.

is probably the most convenient option for South Island snorkellers; the rich band of kelp that hugs the length of the breakwater offers almost a kilometre of opportunity.

Anemones

The constant surf and swell of the Pacific Northwest offer a veritable banquet for sea anemones, as the waves deliver breakfast, lunch and dinner directly to their hungry maws. Snorkellers love the eruptions of underwater colour that burst forth from the larger varieties such as the rose and giant green surf anemones, dramatic fields of giant plumose, as well as the dainty tentacles and translucent pastels of the more diminutive species.

- **Iron Mine Bay** and **Aylard Farm** in East Sooke Park both host abundant, large rose anemones and green surf anemones, which thrive in the constant swell generic to the Juan de Fuca Strait.
- In addition to harbouring rose and green surf anemones, **Silver Spray Beach** (East Sooke) has a healthy population of white-spotted rose anemones (which generally tend to be rarer than the non-spotted variety). Silver Spray is also replete with stubby rose anemones, which you will find at the rock-sand interface. If you have timed your visit with slack tide and the current feels manageable, extend your excursion to include Possession Point—there are patches of strawberry anemones at relatively shallow depths (3–5 metres) and several colonies of giant plumose anemones.
- **Argonaut Wharf** (Campbell River) is anemone central!

Anemone mouth parts are a favourite close-up for underwater photographers.

The wharf's pilings are literally coated with both giant and short plumose, with plenty of painted anemones around as well. In addition to the common white variety, some of the plumose here are a deep orange colour. There are also a few crimson anemones deeper down, but these require dives of at least 5 metres, depending on the tide height.

Sunflower stars and rose anemones are common sights at Aylard Farm.

- **Echo Bay** (Saturna Island) is one of the very best locations to experience a massive giant plumose anemone colony at snorkel-friendly depths. Indeed, at moderately low tide, they will be at eye level, so you don't even need to dive for them. There are also stubby rose anemones to enjoy in the shallows at the rock-sand interface closer to the beach.
- Tilly Point at **Craddock Beach** (Pender Island) equals the abundance of giant plumose observable at Echo Bay, but is more accessible in terms of both the walk-in and the swim required to reach the colonies. The main drawbacks of this location are the strong current and the slightly greater depths of the anemone spectacle. Craddock Beach is therefore rewarding for the more experienced snorkeller.
- **Tralee Point** (Hornby Island) is jam-packed with moonglow anemones, and you don't even need to get wet to enjoy them!

The low rock shelves offer ideal tide-pool viewing even for the non-snorkeller, but for the full spectacle, enjoy the bay in front of the cabins at any tide level.

- **Plumper Wall** in the North Island is fairly covered with small plumose anemones in both white and orange colour morphs; I liken this location to a scaled-down version of Browning Wall (see below). But Plumper Wall's main ticket onto this hit list is the frequency of both crimson anemones (at very accessible depths)

Every inch of space on Browning Wall is covered with anemones.

and brooding anemones. Make sure to look carefully at the base of the brooding anemones, which will often host tiny young that cluster around their trunk, leading to their maternal moniker.

- Saving the best till last: **Browning Wall** (Nigei Island), the undisputed capital of cnidarian country! The entire cliff face is coated with anemones as far as the eye can see, with nary an uninhabited chink in the high-density living. Mostly these are of the plumose variety, but there are also plenty of painted and green surf anemones to boot.

Family Outings

Does your spouse groan every time you reach for your snorkel? Are your kids neglected as a result of your underwater habit? Does your dog look wistfully at you, recalling a time when you took her for walks on the beach, instead of striding into the ocean? Never fear—there are plenty of locations to keep the whole family happy.

- **Fonyo Beach** is my recommendation for a downtown Victoria family outing. While you are exploring the offshore reefs, your family can enjoy a range of activities at Beacon Hill Park: flower gardens, roaming peacocks, springtime flower meadows, the world's largest free-standing totem pole, and of course the petting zoo. Tourists will want to take the obligatory photo at Mile 0 of the Trans-Canada Highway and the Terry Fox memorial. Finally (and, I would venture, most importantly), the Beacon Drive-In serves monster ice creams and other treats year-round.
- In nearby Esquimalt, **Saxe Point Park** boasts a large, grassy area that is ideal for family groups. Woodland trails around the park are perfect for a pre-picnic stroll. Washrooms, picnic tables, plentiful parking and easy city access (including convenient transit stops) make this another in-town winner for Victoria families.
- **Aylard Farm** (East Sooke Park) is perennially popular with families, thanks to its easy access, facilities and wide, sandy beach. Enjoy the hiking trails, picnic tables and fine sandy coastline that is close enough to the car park to launch kayaks and paddleboards with minimal fuss.
- **East Point** (Saturna Island) makes for an ideal family day out in the Gulf Islands. The kiddies can enjoy the fine shell shoreline and calm, crystal waters at Trillium Beach, safely indulging in their own water fun. Adults in the party will appreciate a visit to the heritage Fog Alarm Building, which has been restored and is open to the public. Finally, enjoy

excellent shore-based wildlife spotting—many seabird varieties, a large sea lion haul-out on Boiling Reef, abundant harbour seals and the chance to see orcas cruise past. There are also picnic tables, washrooms and easy parking.

- **Neck Point Park** is one of the best family-friendly destinations in the Nanaimo area. There is an extensive shoreline to stroll around, including scrambles over volcanic rocks for the kiddies, several kilometres of forest trails for shade-seekers, and pebble coves for the more sedentary. Good parking, portable toilets and numerous benches dot the park. Kayak and paddleboard launching is also easy from the beach next to the parking lot. Finally, Neck Point is close to several other parks (such as Pipers Lagoon and Linley Valley), should your family members want to strike out on some further venturing.

- A family camping trip to **Pachena Bay** on the West Coast is always a winner. The massive expanse of sandy beach lends itself to all manner of seaside activities, from Frisbee to soccer and sandcastles. The gentle surf that laps the sand is perfect for youngsters to frolic in, but the bay itself is usually calm enough for those wanting to swim, kayak or paddleboard. A cruise along the western shoreline, with its numerous undercut "caves," is a good bet for spotting black bears poking around for a snack.

- Botanical Beach is a fabulous day trip that is approximately equidistant from both Nanaimo and Victoria. While you are enjoying a swim at **Botany Bay**, the non-snorkellers in your party can get a teaser taster of the underwater bounty by cruising the tide pools that have been scoured out by millennia of ocean action. If beach exploration is not their thing, there are some 50 kilometres of oceanfront hiking trails that should keep them busy.

Beginners

When taking out newbie snorkellers, I try to keep several factors in mind. Primarily, I want them to have a fun and safe experience so that they will be motivated to come back. This means identifying a location where they will see some eye-popping wildlife while feeling protected from currents and swell. Beginners often have yet to purchase a weight belt, or will feel uncomfortable diving more than a few metres, so the critter show also has to be happening on a relatively shallow stage. Beginners are also often lacking fins—further reason to avoid higher-current areas or destinations that require a longer swim.

- **Ogden Point Breakwater** (Greater Victoria) is a great place for beginners, particularly if you stick to the inside wall at the far end.
- **Iron Mine Bay** (East Sooke Park) is another location that offers superlative snorkelling for all levels. The main downside of bringing beginners here: you will have set the bar extremely high, as this is one of the best (easily accessible) snorkel locations on Vancouver Island!
- **Terrace Beach** (Ucluelet) offers a sampling of the wild West Coast, while remaining protected from the waves that famously batter most of the region's shores. You'll find abundant nudibranchs, sea stars and anemones all along both rocky shores and moon snails in the shallows. Avoid the summer, though, as the bay is socked in with vegetation.
- **Peter Cove** on Pender Island is possibly one of the very best options for the beginner snorkeller. First, it is very well protected from wind, swell and current. Second, water entry from the shallow pebble beach is easy. Third, the bay and its rocky foreshore are all relatively shallow and do not demand any significant diving ability.
- **Telegraph Cove** (Greater Victoria) is another location where flat, calm waters are the norm and strong currents (as long as you stay in the bay) are non-existent. Combine these

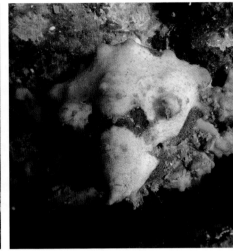

Puget Sound king crabs are colourful as both adults (left) and juveniles (right).

benevolent water conditions with shallow depths, plentiful parking, a short walk to the beach and an easy water entry, and you have all of the elements for a happy beginner.

- At **Clover Point** (Greater Victoria), newbies will be pretty much guaranteed to see nudibranchs (as long as they don't come at the height of summer, when everything is covered in vegetation) and a variety of sea stars, anemones and crustaceans.

- The **Dyer Rocks** in the Saanich Inlet are ideal for beginners in several respects. In addition to the protected location and shallow depths, the summertime water temperature can reach a balmy 18°C or so, making for a much more comfortable experience if you don't yet have a fancy open cell wetsuit.

Freediving

In this book I have deliberately focused on locations that will appeal to the snorkeller whose dives will take them no deeper than around 5–10 metres. But for those who like to plumb the depths, many of the locations in this book offer more challenging diving. Of course, simply by swimming out from shore one can access arbitrarily deeper terrain, but the locations listed here offer precipitous drop-offs that allow you to get deep without straying far from land.

- **Cliffside** (Saturna Island)—the clue is in the name. These south-facing cliffs are sheer enough that orcas cruise just a stone's throw from the shoreline.
- While most of the snorkelling terrain at **Iron Mine Bay** is less than 10 metres deep and feels fairly protected, as you approach the far end of the cliffs to the south, the depths beneath you start to open up. Exploring here requires the conditions to be calm, both in terms of inherent swell and the wind (which will likely be coming from around the point).
- **Argonaut Wharf** is an ideal location for perfecting your freediving skills while marvelling at the anemones that coat the pilings from surface to sea floor. As long as you have timed your dive correctly to coincide

The pilings at Argonaut Wharf are covered with life.

with slack water (see page 178 for tips on how to do this), you can enjoy peaceful dives, knowing that the sea floor is a mere 15 metres below (rather than feeling the unease of the gaping abyss that goes with many dives on walls). Arrival at the sea floor may be rewarded with a sighting of a giant dendronotid hunting for the tube-dwelling anemones that inhabit the sandy bottom.

- **Ten Mile Point** is one of Victoria's premier scuba diving locations, thanks to the steep wall that drops off for many tens of metres at the end of White Rock Street. Beware the current.
- The **Ogden Point Breakwater** is another well-known Victoria scuba diving location. Its construction from metre-high concrete blocks, staggered like those of Egyptian step pyramids, means that the depth descends in a nicely incremental fashion. How deep you go is therefore essentially a choose-your-own-adventure, with a mini-plateau every metre.
- **Northeast Pearse Island** pays dividends if you can get yourself a bit deeper. The main shelf leading out from the island bottoms out at about 7 or 8 metres, before turning down into a steep wall about 20 metres from the shore, beyond the kelp bed. Near the top of the wall, you will see an avalanche of short plumose anemones descending into the deep. Scuba divers report that going farther down the wall opens up a colourful canvas of sponges and hydrocorals, but I'll have to take their word for it.

Boat Outings

One of the joys of snorkelling is that, compared with scuba diving, it requires only simple shoreline access and relatively little specialist equipment. Indeed, most of the destinations in this guide are easily accessible by road, with only a short walk-in required. However, I have included some entries that require boat access;

sometimes this can be as simple as a kayak, but others benefit from powered craft. Here are my top picks for those who can be mobile.

- The **Pachena Bay Islets** offer a first-class day trip for snorkellers equipped with kayaks. If you still have the energy after your snorkelling, you can continue your paddle around the coastline, but give the reefs a wide berth, as breakers pound the rocks even on calm days. A further 3-kilometre paddle takes you to Keeha Beach, a 2-kilometre-long sandy crescent within Pacific Rim National Park.
- A scuttled BC ferry, the **May Island** wreck is a short boat ride from Campbell River (or Quathiaski Cove on Quadra Island) and offers the combination of interesting terrain and good species diversity. Although the approach is short, a powered craft is preferable to kayaks, given the strong currents that seem to be omnipresent through Discovery Passage.
- Although **Cabin Point**, in East Sooke Park, can certainly be reached on foot, the hike in can be pretty tedious when you're carrying all of your gear. Fortunately, the presence of a perfect pocket beach, set back from the main ocean swell, makes an ideal landing or anchorage for small motor vessels.
- **Browning Wall** is the ultimate snorkel destination in this guide, but also the most logistically challenging to reach. There is no beach or place to anchor, so you'll need a live boat (i.e., someone left onboard). It's also a fair distance from the closest town (Port Hardy), and the waters here can be feisty. So it's highly recommended that you approach Browning Wall in someone else's vessel, i.e., by dive charter.
- **Plumper Wall** is not only a world-class destination, but with a powered craft it is in easy reach of places like Telegraph Cove and Alert Bay. There is no beach here, but there are a few spots where you can improvise a tie-up to the shore (or better, have a live boat).

The Pachena Bay Islets are a perfect kayak destination.

- The **Masterman Islands** are one of the few places in the North Island section of this book that can be readily reached by kayak. The paddle out through Hardy Bay is relatively protected and you can stick close to shore for all but the final short section that crosses to the archipelago. The fine crushed-shell coves and shallow, sandy bays along some of the inner shores make for excellent landing sites.

WHEN TO SNORKEL AROUND VANCOUVER ISLAND

The reality is that you can enjoy snorkelling year-round in BC waters. However, there are several factors that will impact both your enjoyment and your safety, including visibility, currents and tides. Here is my potted summary of annual considerations for snorkelling around Vancouver Island.

January–February

Cooler air temperatures frighten away all but the hardiest of souls, but with a good wetsuit you can stay warm throughout the winter. Wind and rain decrease water visibility around the South Island, and strong swells pound the exposed West Coast. On the other hand, there is little plankton and algae to cloud the water. Areas around Nanaimo and Campbell River offer some of the better winter visibility—profiting from their protected aspect, and being out of the west winds. For South Islanders, the Saanich Inlet (cursed by organic soup in the spring and summer) also offers a more protected locale with visibility that can outperform Victoria's shoreline. Daytime low tides are largely absent in January, meaning that the snorkeller has to look (or dive) through an extra couple of metres of water column, but by February, some late-afternoon low tides are creeping back into the calendar (but are highly location dependent). On the other hand, if the water is clear, you can still soak up the surface views, seek out shallow locations and enjoy the eye-level ecosystems of docks and buoys. Location tips: Since Argonaut Wharf requires high-tide timing in order to avoid the strong back eddies, winter is a great time of year to check it out. Visiting the Royston shipwrecks also benefits from higher tides.

March–May

By March, daytime low tides have returned around the island, exposing a wider range of wildlife without the need to dive very deep. Indeed, March can be a sweet spot for snorkellers as vegetation has yet to gain a real foothold, so much of the shoreline is still exposed, and critters are easy to spot. However, by the end of March, kelp and vegetation start to regrow as the sunlight increases in daily length and intensity. Rocks that were exposed through the winter, offering an unimpeded view of their inhabitants, begin to grow over, and by the middle of April much of the South Island shoreline is covered in seaweeds. March and April also mark a rapid deterioration of visibility in the Saanich Inlet and along the central east coast. The Strait of Georgia is additionally affected by the herring spawn; while the sight of billions of fish is an unforgettable snorkel experience (try Hornby Island), thick clouds of roe will soon reduce visibility to zero. Indeed, the March–May period is notorious as one of the poorer visibility stretches of the year around much of the island. On the plus side, the swells on the outer coast start to decrease, offering calmer waters along the Sooke coastline, and there are some good visibility days to be had from March onward. Spring is also a fabulous time for enjoying the massive number of tiny jellies that inhabit the upper water layers—almost anywhere you snorkel in April and May will deliver a myriad of species in a seemingly limitless variety of bizarre shapes.

June–August

The summer months are likely when you'll feel inspired to do most of your snorkelling. By June, the water temperature is

Pacific herring gather in massive numbers in mid-to-late March to spawn.

starting to creep up, and in mid-island locales you may even be able to submerge without a neoprene coating by July. However, in the summer months many locations are fairly covered with leafy vegetation, which hampers wildlife viewing. The water visibility is also still highly variable in the early half of the summer, with murky waters potentially persisting into June and July in plankton-rich years. On the plus side, phosphorescent species light up waters around the island to put on a nightly spectacle, perfect for an evening dip. My two favourite locations for enjoying a bioluminescent night snorkel are Coles Bay (North Saanich) and Drew Harbour (Quadra Island), the latter of which enjoys water warm enough to take your midnight swim *au naturel* (or at least, sans neoprene). By mid-August, the visibility is consistently improving, and the second half of the month offers (Mother

Swarms of jellies often get trapped in protected bays and are a common sight in spring and summer.

Nature willing) a great combination of daytime low tides, long days, good weather and great visibility. The North Island, with its brief summer season, is best visited in these months for the above-water conditions (although even at this point the weather is unpredictable).

September–October

My favourite time of the year to snorkel! Still plenty of sunlight and daytime low tides, and the kelp and vegetation have started to die back around the South Island. This is a magic combination of exposed surfaces and low water levels that reveals wild-life readily to the snorkeller. Visibility can be excellent in these months around Victoria, the Gulf Islands and the Sooke coastline, since the swell is still low and populations of algae and plankton are largely absent. Low visibility days in the fall are most likely to be driven by wind and rain. Fall and early winter also bring generally the best visibility in the Strait of Georgia, whose location in the lee of the prevailing west winds also tends to offer more protection. September is also generally considered the sweet spot for North Island adventures, such as in Browning Pass and around the Broughtons—the weather has yet to turn full-on foul, but the legendary visibility days have started to make their appearance. Although the 100-foot visibility persists through the winter, topside weather makes boating adventures less appealing beyond November (and charters often stop running by the end of October). If you intend to book a dive charter, then plan ahead, as scuba divers will snap up the boats up to a year in advance.

November–December

Cooler air temperatures and cloudier days can sap the snorkeller's motivation to suit up and get wet, and storms in the Pacific will start to degrade the water clarity along the West Coast. On the other hand, the visibility along the east coast and the Saanich Inlet can be excellent through the winter, and November offers some not-too-bad low-ish tides in many locations. Sheltered locations will provide calm water that can remain clear if out of the wind, so consult regularly with your preferred weather oracle to scope out the leeward locales. Head to destinations in the Strait of Georgia and around Campbell River for better visibility if southern waters have started to suffer from churning storms, but be aware that daytime tide heights from mid-November till early March can be 4–5 metres along the east coast.

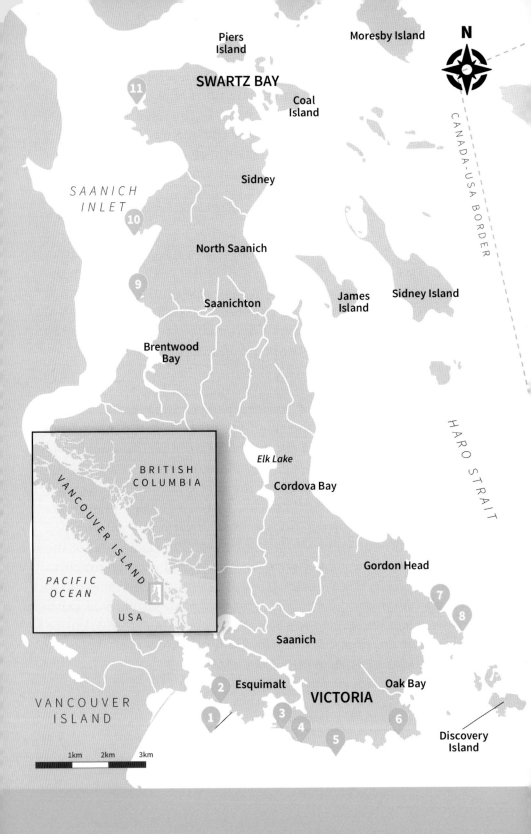

GREATER VICTORIA

1 SAXE POINT PARK and the GILLINGHAM ISLANDS ⭐

Saxe Point Park is a popular urban destination, thanks to its open grassy areas, picnic tables and trail network. The outer trail that runs the circumference of the point is about a kilometre long, with many additional paths criss-crossing the interior. The southwestern aspect makes this a particularly lovely afternoon picnic spot. All told, there is plenty to keep your land-based support crew occupied while you take a dip. Looking southeast, back toward Macaulay Point, the Gillingham Islands are a small cluster of islets about 200 metres offshore.

The underwater topography of Saxe Point is quite appealing to the snorkeller. Close to shore there are some shallow cliffs, undercuts and shelves to explore, as well as pleasant kelp groves in the summertime. Farther out from shore there are deeper walls that also make this a popular spot for scuba divers. All the usual species can be readily found here, although neither the diversity nor the abundance are particularly noteworthy at snorkel depths. However, I find the Gillingham Islands to be generally richer in aquatic life and with more interesting terrain.

The outside wall of the most northern of the Gillingham Islands is fairly shallow and often quite replete with nudibranchs. The short channel between the two main islands has a shallow, sandy bottom that is popular with stubby rose anemones. Take your time checking out the undercuts on the southeast channel wall, where you will find short plumose anemones and often several species of nudibranchs hanging out (or hiding in the many crevices). The outside edge of the more southern island (i.e., farther from Saxe Point) offers the deepest terrain, with a fairly vertical drop down to about 7 metres. There are also several smaller islands a little to the south that offer deeper terrain worth exploring. I have had some satisfying finds here, such as a cushion star, a sunflower star and a Cockerell's dorid. I regularly get checked out by seals in this general area, and sometimes otters too.

Clown nudibranch.

Signature species

All sorts of nudibranchs! I will regularly clock six or seven species on a single visit. Clowns are particularly common all around the Gillingham Islands.

Critter list

Leather star, ochre star, blood star, sunflower star, cushion star, armpit blood star, drab six-armed star, mottled star, giant California sea cucumber, orange sea cucumber, Hudson's dorid, Monterey dorid, Nanaimo dorid, opalescent nudibranch, clown nudibranch, Cockerell's dorid, leopard dorid, white-and-orange-tipped nudibranch, frosted nudibranch, shiny sea squirt, short plumose anemone, giant plumose anemone, stubby rose anemone, rose anemone, white-spotted rose anemone, moon jelly, red urchin, purple urchin, giant Pacific chiton, black leather chiton, lined chiton, kelp greenling, northern staghorn bryozoan.

Access

Access to Saxe Point Park is along Fraser Street. There is abundant parking, as well as park facilities such as washrooms and picnic tables that make this an excellent excursion for the whole family. From the parking lot, it is a short walk to your choice of entry point. My preferred option is to go in directly off the point, largely because I am usually heading across to the Gillingham Islands and I want the shortest possible swim. From the point, there are several sloping rock shelves that are fairly easy to navigate, although this depends a little on the tide height; when the water level is on the lower side, you will be picking your way through fields of barnacles. If you don't fancy the rocks, a beach on the north side offers an easier entry (but potentially a long swim, depending on where you are headed). Finally, with a slightly longer walk from the car park, you can alternatively make your way to the bay between Saxe Point and Royal Point.

Tips

Beware of boat traffic entering the nearby marina. If you are sticking close to the shore, this is unlikely to be a problem, but vessels often cut between Royal Point and the Gillingham Islands. Make the crossing with your buddy, preferably with a buoy, and pop your head up every few fin kicks.

By mid-April, this location is heavily vegetated and spotting the wildlife becomes hard work. The channel between the two main Gillingham Islands also becomes choked with greenery, making even a swim-through challenging. You'll spend most of your time either diving down to find small, exposed rock walls or turning over lots of kelp leaves. Personally, I find this rather unsatisfying, and keep this as a prime in-town location for fall excursions.

FOSTER STREET COVE/ DENNISTON PARK

2

West of Saxe Point Park, before you get to the verboten area of the Esquimalt naval base (where submarines patrol with torpedoes at the ready in the event of any covert nudibranch counting), there are several small coves and public beach access points. Take your pick of southbound streets leading off Esquimalt Road and you'll hit the water within a few blocks. Foster Street Cove is the last bay before the naval base and can be accessed from the end of either Foster Street (east side) or Grafton Street (west side), at the end of which is Denniston Park. The description of this area as a public park is rather an overstatement; it is actually just a tiny piece of tree-shaded grass with a couple of picnic tables, and then a short, rocky point.

For snorkelling, you have two main options: the cove or the south-facing rocky shoreline to its west. The cove itself is only about 70 metres across and not very deep. On a good visibility day, you will be able to see the sandy shingle bottom. There is not much living in the central part of the bay, and you'll likely want to concentrate your explorations on the rocky boundaries. Wildlife in the shallows here is fairly sparse, a few lonely anemones and sea stars, although the cove is protected and will feel safe for beginners.

The rocky shoreline off the point of Denniston Park is both considerably richer in wildlife and more interesting in the terrain department. Although the drop-off is not steep or deep, there are lots of big boulders that extend to depths of 5–7 metres. In the summer, there is a rich kelp forest anchored on these rocks, and

Rose anemones can have variously coloured crowns, but their trunks are always a uniform ruby.

the stipes remain well into the winter. However, the point is more open to swell and current, and the novice snorkeller may feel a tad exposed. The Brothers Islands look temptingly close from here, but be aware that these are located a stone's throw from the naval base, and your presence may generate some unwanted attention.

Signature species

Although common along the Sooke coast, rose anemones are not too common in Victoria's urban waters. Denniston Park is one of the spots around the provincial capital where you will find them in abundance.

Critter list

Mottled star, ochre star, blood star, armpit blood star, sunflower star, drab six-armed star, leather star, rose anemone, painted anemone, stubby rose anemone, pink-tipped aggregating anemone, green surf anemone, brooding anemone, kelp greenling, Pacific herring, fried egg jelly, giant Pacific chiton, orange sea cucumber, giant California sea cucumber, shiny sea squirt, giant rock scallop, northern abalone, noble sea lemon, Monterey dorid, leopard dorid, clown nudibranch, Nanaimo dorid, red urchin, umbrella crab, smoothhead sculpin.

Access

Despite several public beach access points, you get the feeling that visitors are discouraged in this neighbourhood. You can cruise street after street and find nothing but Residential Parking Only signs. The most convenient parking access for Foster Street Cove is at the end of Grafton Street, where you can find a measly four parking spots huddled around the small turnaround at the end of the road.

If you manage to secure one of these coveted parking spots (I exaggerate: I have actually always been able to sneak in—possibly, most visitors are indeed put off by the less-than-welcoming street signage), the walk is short, just 50 metres or so along a paved path to the rocky tip of Denniston Park. Water access can be tricky, as the drop-off is quite steep. At high tide, your entry will be over fairly smooth rock, and you can just plop in. At low tide, you'll be scrambling down over barnacles. Getting out is probably the trickier part, particularly if there is any swell.

3 OGDEN POINT BREAKWATER

Located in the James Bay district of Victoria, the Ogden Point Breakwater extends almost a kilometre out from Dallas Road, making it a popular strolling spot for locals and visitors alike. Within easy reach of the downtown core and numerous residential neighbourhoods, the breakwater is also well-trod by the passengers that pour out of the adjacent cruise ship terminal in the summertime. The small, sandy beach below is a favourite with local families, and a recent renovation of the area has seen the installation of lounge-style chairs and large community picnic tables along the Dallas Road promenade.

In terms of its underwater delights, the breakwater is *the* classic destination in Victoria for scuba divers, and a pretty good one for snorkellers as well, especially at low tide. For most of the year, there is a considerable kelp forest on the outside edge of the breakwater, which is lovely to swim through while you're looking for critters, but it does make manoeuvring a bit more challenging. This kelp growth is thick enough that it takes most of the winter to significantly die back, so early spring is a good time to snorkel here, combining daytime low tides and less kelp. Conversely, the inside edge of the breakwater is kelp-free year-round and has the additional benefit of offering protection from current, wind and waves. The inner breakwater is therefore a great spot for beginners, and still has plenty to see, including sea cucumbers, urchins, tube worms, scallops, nudibranchs and chitons. However, you should stick close to the wall and not venture too far in, else you risk a stern (and justified) telling-off from the harbour master.

Lacking external gills, the white berthella is not a nudibranch.

Signature species

Vermilion stars and striped sunstars are both frequent sights on the outside wall and you can find larger species such as ling-cod and Puget Sound king crab in the top 5 metres or so. There is a large-ish colony of giant plumose anemones at 7–10 metres depth between the first bend (as you leave from the beach) and the stairs. On a clear visibility day, these are just about visible from the surface. In late September and early October, search for hooded nudibranchs (and their egg ribbons) on kelp fronds.

Critter list

Giant plumose anemone, short plumose anemone, rose anemone, painted anemone, purple urchin, green urchin, red urchin, cushion star, striped sunstar, vermilion star, ochre star, leather star, blood star, sunflower star, giant California sea cucumber, orange sea cucumber, armoured sea cucumber, pale sea cucumber, clown nudibranch, hooded nudibranch, white berthella, Monterey dorid, noble sea lemon, yellow margin dorid, Puget Sound king crab, black leather chiton, giant Pacific chiton, lined chiton, pink scallop, giant rock scallop, northern abalone, calcareous tube worm, Pacific herring, kelp greenling, lingcod, cabezon, copper rockfish.

Access

Parking for Ogden Point is along Dallas Road, although you might be hard-pressed to find a spot when the weather is nice. The alternative is either to pay for parking behind the Breakwater Café (free on Sunday) or to search out street parking on the nearby residential streets (while checking carefully for Resident Only signs).

Once you're parked, water entry is either from the beach below the café or at one of the stairs along (or at the end of) the breakwater. The beach is by far the easiest, but the sea life becomes more varied as you venture out along the wall. If you plan to snorkel the inner wall, you should definitely use the stairs at the far end; otherwise, it is a long swim and you may be battling current at the point. Scuba divers will tell you that the best wildlife is at the far end, but for the snorkeller, once around the first bend (from the beach) it is all pretty similar on the outer wall.

Tips

Entry from the breakwater itself is from huge granite blocks—if there is surge, this can be a little tricky to say the least. Many a diver has abandoned all pretense of decorum in their attempts to both enter and exit the water. The blocks are also quite barnacled, so I prefer to wear my hard-soled booties and plastic fins here.

Watch out for fishing line—always dive with a knife in the unlikely event that you get snagged. Despite the omnipresence of fisherfolk on the breakwater itself, harvesting from within the water (i.e., while you are snorkelling or diving) is forbidden at this location.

FONYO BEACH

4

Located between Clover Point and Ogden Point, Fonyo Beach is a wide sweep of pebble shoreline popular with beach walkers and families. The green space above the beach is Holland Point Park, whose five-hectare area splits the Dallas Road esplanade into a scenic loop. Holland Point Park is a pleasant family destination in its own right—on a nice day the boating pond is replete with model yachts, and kiddies can enjoy the small playground area (and feeding the ducks).

The main snorkelling attraction at Fonyo Beach is a set of shallow rocks extending out from the beach, ending in a small reef about 150 metres offshore. The reef is exposed at low tide, but completely submerged when water levels are high in the wintertime. You might just about intuit the rocks' location by the presence of small breakers cresting their peaks. In the summer, the entire area is chock full of bull kelp, which usually subsides by mid-November.

The swim out to the reef is fairly shallow, no more than about 5 metres deep, even at relatively high tide. The underwater terrain is mixed sand and rock, with a few larger boulders whose undersides merit closer inspection for anemones, nudibranchs and tunicates. The reef itself is thickly covered by barnacles and large California mussels, as well as colourful coralline algae and splashes of red sponges. There is a good range of nudibranchs to be found here. Sea stars are abundant, although the species variety is rather limited. Beyond the reef, the water gets a little deeper, but even here the drop-off is very gradual.

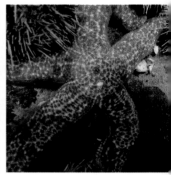

Mottled stars display a range of colours.

Critter list

Purple urchin, red urchin, orange sea cucumber, stiff-footed sea cucumber, shiny sea squirt, winged sea slug, comb jelly, cross jelly, moon jelly, black leather chiton, giant rock scallop, California mussel, blood star, armpit blood star, leather star, mottled star, drab six-armed star, colourful six-armed star, painted anemone, rose anemone, stubby rose anemone, kelp greenling, Monterey dorid, Heath's dorid, Nanaimo dorid, noble sea lemon, leopard dorid, clown nudibranch, frosted nudibranch.

Access

The path down to Fonyo Beach starts from Dallas Road, between Paddon and Olympia avenues. Parking here can be a little tricky, particularly if the weather is nice and folks are out enjoying a beach stroll. There is some limited parallel parking on the north (non-water) side of Dallas Road. There are more spaces at the top of Holland Point Park, near the boating lake on the ocean side. Most of the streets that branch off Dallas Road are for residents only, so if you can't score a spot at either of the aforementioned places, the next best option is farther east along Dallas Road, just south of Beacon Hill; it's about a 400-metre walk back to the Fonyo Beach trail from here.

From Dallas Road, you can easily see Fonyo Beach below (there is a sign more or less at the end of Paddon Avenue). A paved path snakes its way down the modest descent, ending in a short set of concrete stairs—about 100 metres in total from the street.

Tips

In the summertime, this section of coastline is thick with bull kelp, which makes navigation a bit of a tricky tangle. I like to come here in the late fall, when the kelp has mostly died back and the last stipes left standing are covered in kelp crabs.

The shallow nature of this site means that it can be enjoyed even at relatively high tide (as long as the visibility is good). Combined with the lack of kelp outside of the summer months, Fonyo Beach is therefore a good wintertime destination. Regardless of the time of year, a stop at the Beacon Drive-In for ice cream is a post-snorkel essential!

5 CLOVER POINT

This south-facing rocky promontory is a great in-town snorkelling option with a species variety that is on a par with the Ogden Point Breakwater. Construction of a sewage pump station in around 2020 resulted in a facelift for Clover Point, replacing the old parking lot with a recreational area, against the backdrop of much community debate. The end result is a grassy area (good), limited parking (not so good, although there is still plenty along Dallas Road), picnic tables and summertime food trucks, as well as a spiffy new washroom and outdoor shower.

To the east of Clover Point is a wide, protected bay that is good for beginners as long as the wind isn't blowing from the south, and as long as one is watchful of the tides (there can be quite a strong pull from the current even inside the bay). Most of the interesting wildlife is close to the rocky shoreline, rather than in the middle of the bay itself. A favourite spot of mine is about 50 metres directly out from the boat ramp, where there are some submerged rocky reefs that extend down to 7 metres or so and are often rich in life.

Alternatively, you can explore around the point itself. You can either stay close to the shore for a surface snorkel (there is a lot to see off the shallow rocks around the tip without the need to dive) or venture a little farther out to dive to depths of 5–10 metres. Again, the current can fairly whip around the point, so snorkel here around low tide to make the most of the slack current and intertidal offerings. I find the bay to the west of the point to be rather devoid of interesting critters.

Giant white dorid.

Signature species
There are always lots of Monterey dorids on the rocks to the right of the boat ramp; indeed, I have usually spotted my first Montereys within minutes of entering. Leopard dorids, frosted nudibranchs, giant white dorids and clown nudibranchs are also common sightings here. I also have pretty good luck with striped sunstars here.

Critter list
Rose anemone, painted anemone, giant plumose anemone, pink-tipped aggregating anemone, brooding anemone, purple urchin,

winged sea slug, fried egg jelly, comb jelly, orange sea cucumber, drab six-armed star, colourful six-armed star, ochre star, mottled star, blood star, armpit blood star, striped sunstar, rainbow star, sunflower star, leather star, frosted nudibranch, Monterey dorid, Heath's dorid, red sponge dorid, noble sea lemon, giant white dorid, clown nudibranch, leopard dorid, San Diego dorid, Nanaimo dorid, yellow margin dorid, northern feather duster worm.

Access

Park at the point itself, on Dallas Road or along one of the nearby residential streets (checking for parking restrictions). For access to the bay, you can either enter at the pebble beach next to Dallas Road or make a short and easy scramble down the rocks at the tip of the point. A third option, and my preferred entry point, is from the Anglers' Association boat ramp, but of course be aware of boat traffic and respectful of the fisherfolk coming and going. In particular, avoid the passage cut in the kelp that shows where the boats transit, as this is essentially akin to swimming on a runway.

Tips

In the summertime, there are food trucks on Dallas Road between Clover Point and Beacon Hill Park (to the west)—post-snorkel tacos, anyone?

KITTY ISLET

6

At the eastern end of McNeill Bay in Greater Victoria's Oak Bay municipality, Kitty Islet is a dainty, rocky peninsula whose narrow waist is flanked by two small pebble beaches. Around the peninsula are several modest outcrops that are variously exposed, depending on the tide height. In the summertime, a thick band of kelp encircles the peninsula and eelgrass turns the shallows an emerald green (come here in winter or early spring for easier critter spotting). Looking out toward the Trial Islands, a pair of south-facing Adirondack chairs offers a wonderful vista across to the Olympic Mountains in Washington state. All in all, Kitty Islet is a magical spot.

For the snorkeller, Kitty Islet has lots of little nooks and crannies to explore, including the pair of shallow bays, multiple rocky outcrops and some sandy channels. Most of the terrain here is at snorkeller-friendly depths of around 5 metres or less. In good visibility and current conditions, exploring a little deeper offshore is satisfying, but be aware of the fact that the water motion can pick up quickly through Enterprise Channel. But it is this current that feeds the ecosystem, and I find Kitty Islet to be one of the more species-diverse locations in Oak Bay. Exposure to the current means that you'll find more anemones here than at most of the places in this chapter, including some beautiful, large rose anemones. There are also plentiful sea stars, including lots of blood stars and the six-armed variety; sunflower stars have also become more frequent here in recent years. You are also highly

Lobed compound tunicate.

likely to find a good collection of nudibranchs—I regularly spot large noble sea lemons here.

Signature species

One of my favourite things about Kitty Islet is the colourful tunicates. The species selection ranges from the solitary shiny sea squirts, which are splattered around like glossy red hearts on the rocks, to gorgeous spreads of social and compound tunicates in a rainbow of shades from ruby to peach.

Critter list

Ochre star, mottled star, blood star, armpit blood star, drab six-armed star, colourful six-armed star, sunflower star, rose anemone, painted anemone, short plumose anemone,

Heart crab.

pink-tipped aggregating anemone, brooding anemone, shiny sea squirt, lobed compound tunicate, black leather chiton, giant Pacific chiton, giant rock scallop, orange sea cucumber, giant California sea cucumber, stiff-footed sea cucumber, Heath's dorid, Monterey dorid, noble sea lemon, multicolour dendronotid, clown nudibranch, frosted nudibranch, leopard dorid, Nanaimo dorid, heart crab, copper rockfish, red urchin, green urchin.

Access

There is easy (but limited) parking on the ocean side of Beach Drive, in a broad pullout right next to the beach entry. Usually, there is sufficient space here that you will find a spot, since Kitty Islet's compact beach does not attract lingering crowds. For the water entry, take your pick from one of two pebble beaches along the isthmus.

Tips

Be very careful with current here. Even at slack tide, I find the current can pick up quickly, so I rarely venture very far from the main rocks unless the visibility is good (so I can keep my bearings) and the water is exhibiting an extended slack.

In my opinion, the most interesting topography is the steeper east-facing wall near the southern beach, as well as the southern point, which allows you to explore farther offshore if the conditions are benign.

This general area (and for several kilometres east) tends to be susceptible to waste-water overflow warnings after heavy rains. Check the Capital Regional District website for alerts (warnings are also posted on signage at the beach).

TELEGRAPH COVE

7

At the northwestern extent of Ten Mile Point, Telegraph Cove offers a moderately large pebble beach and sheltered, north-facing cove. The combination of its sheltered aspect, easy water access, plentiful parking and short walk-in makes it popular with kayak launchers and families alike. It rarely gets truly busy here (nearby Cadboro Bay is the bigger local crowd-puller), but if seclusion is your thing, know that you are likely to be sharing this beach with other groups.

In the summer, the sea floor and rocky shoreline are covered in vegetation and there is not much to see, unless you have the saint-like patience required to part every leaf in search of inverte-brate life. However, once the vegetation dies back, usually by early October, this bay becomes a decent Victoria spot, particu-larly for lovers of shallow locations safe from cur-rents and boat traffic. The rocky shore to the left of the beach offers the best

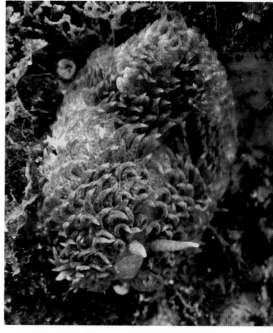

Shag-rug (shaggy mouse) nudibranch.

Branched dendronotid.

abundance and diversity of life, and this is a particularly good stretch for nudibranchs. The waters here also seem to be conducive to gathering jelly life, in particular fried egg jellies, which can accumulate in significant numbers in the late summer and early fall. However, the lack of open ocean exposure and deeper waters means that bigger sea life (such as surf-loving anemones and larger sea star species) is largely absent here.

Critter list

Fried egg jelly, comb jelly, short plumose anemone, painted anemone, pink-tipped aggregating anemone, orange sea cucumber, shiny sea squirt, ochre star, mottled star, blood star, leather star, drab six-armed star, yellow margin dorid, Hudson's dorid, Nanaimo dorid, clown nudibranch, branched dendronotid, Monterey dorid, Heath's dorid, shag-rug nudibranch, northern clingfish.

Access

There is fairly plentiful parking at the end of Telegraph Bay Road, though the popularity of this spot in high summer means that it can start to feel a little crowded. From the parking lot, it is a very short walk to the beach. Water entry is easy—a shallow, sloping pebble beach that rarely experiences any significant wave action.

Tips

There are several mooring buoys in the bay that have some interesting wildlife growing on the underside, including shiny sea squirts, short plumose anemones and calcareous tube worms. If the visibility is lousy, you'll still be able to spend a happy few moments on the surface perusing these little microclimates.

The north-facing aspect of Telegraph Cove, combined with its western location, means that it is often protected from prevailing winds. I have experienced calm waters here, even when the waves are lashing Dallas Road.

8 SPRING BAY / TEN MILE POINT

At the northeastern end of the Ten Mile Point peninsula, Spring Bay is just west of the classic "wall" scuba site, and a popular secondary dive location in its own right. This bay is also great for snorkellers—it is relatively shallow and has a few underwater shelves that make for interesting terrain. Spring Bay is a good spot for nudibranchs, and hosts lots of sea cucumbers (both orange and giant California) that make the sea floor colourful in the spring-time. The main drawback to this location is the visibility, which seems to rarely be as good as some of the other Greater Victoria locations in this guide. The whole area also gets kelpy and vege-tated by late spring, and so is best visited in early spring or fall.

For those wanting to explore more of the peninsula, the point at the end of White Rock Street (which is the main scuba site) has some deeper rocky shelves (before plunging down the dive wall) that are frequented by large ochre and mottled stars. You can also follow the shoreline around to the right (south) toward Baynes Beach. Indeed, connecting Baynes Beach and Ten Mile Point is a good option if the current is up and you can do a point-to-point drift snorkel (retracing your steps topside along White Rock Street).

Signature species

There are regular sightings of Cockerell's dorids at Spring Bay, and the frosted nudibranchs are consistently some of the largest and most spectacular that I have seen.

A pair of mating Cockerell's dorids.

Critter list

Orange sea cucumber, giant California sea cucumber, pale sea cucumber, shiny sea squirt, painted anemone, pink-tipped aggregating anemone, giant plumose anemone, black leather chiton, lined chiton, giant Pacific chiton, leopard dorid, Heath's dorid, Hudson's dorid, frosted nudibranch, Cockerell's dorid, clown nudibranch, mottled star, drab six-armed star, blood star, green urchin, red urchin, purple urchin.

Access

There are two ways to access Spring Bay. The first option is to enter from the west, achieved by parking at the far end of Tudor

Avenue, where there is a small turnaround with space for half a dozen cars (note the Emergency/No Parking signs at the very end). The water entrance here is easy, via a small pebble beach, but the swim to the point is longer (albeit through the nice bay area). Alternatively, park at the far end of White Rock Street. This is where the scuba divers jump in, so it may be preferable for those interested in freediving down the wall rather than snorkelling in the bay. But sharing this entry with scuba divers means that it can be busier here, and car parking is limited. Beyond the busier parking, the main downside to the White Rock Street approach is that the water entry and exit are much trickier here. In contrast to the easy pebble beach at the west end of the bay, from White Rock Street you have to make a short scramble down over some fairly rugged rocks (bring your hard-soled booties and beater fins). The point is also much more exposed to current, so snorkelling at the east end of the bay requires judicious timing with slack tide (more on this below). Overall, I prefer the ease of the Tudor Avenue entry.

Tips

Ten Mile Point is famous for the strong currents that shred around the corner, and divers know to come here only at slack tide. Snorkellers should definitely aim for slack *low* tide to enjoy the shallow bay area, though this is generally a bit more protected than the undersea wall at the end of White Rock Street. Conventional wisdom among local divers is to use the current and tide prediction site dairiki.org to forecast slack tide by subtracting 15 minutes from the time of zero current exchange at Race Passage. Once you have this location-corrected slack tide time, you can enjoy fairly still waters for 30 minutes or so. The timing is less critical the farther west you are in the bay.

HENDERSON POINT

9

Henderson Point is one of three popular Saanich Inlet scuba dive sites (the others being Willis Point and McKenzie Bight), thanks to the steep wall that drops vertically just a few dozen metres offshore. There is no real beach here, and the public water access is no more than a rocky interlude between waterfront residences. As a result, Henderson Point is really just a way to get in the water, and definitely not a place to bring companions to enjoy a seashore experience while you are diving.

The compact foreshore is rocky and fairly easy to navigate, sloping gently off into a mix of rocks and sandy patches. The wildlife here is pretty much the same set of offerings found all along the inlet: plenty of sea stars, sea cucumbers, crabs and tunicates, though the species diversity is rather limited. If you head to the right, you will have the option to continue your exploration into Thompson Cove, where you'll find a series of boat docks covered in short plumose anemones, a variety of shellfish and the occasional sea star. It is tempting to swim out and look for the lip of the scuba site drop-off in search of more interesting critters, but this turndown is deep enough that even seeing the top of the wall requires superior visibility and freediving skills.

Critter list

Leather star, ochre star, mottled star, drab six-armed star, giant pink star, Nanaimo dorid, Hudson's dorid, shiny sea squirt, lightbulb tunicate, lined compound tunicate, orange sea cucumber,

67

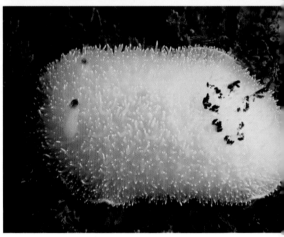

These three small dorids can be hard to tell apart. The Hudson's dorid (top left) has long, hair-like tubercles; the yellow margin dorid's tubercles (top right) are more like small bumps; and the Nanaimo dorid (right) has brown tips on its rhinophores and branchial plume.

pale sea cucumber, giant rock scallop, short plumose anemone, blackeye goby, Pacific herring, gaper clam, black leather chiton.

Access

Senanus Drive is an extension of Mount Newton Cross Road that comes to a dead end where it hits the water at Henderson Point. The road widens at the end to allow cars to turn around, and there is parking for 10 or so vehicles if you use the verges creatively. At the end of the road, a short and obvious trail leads down to the water between houses. Emerging from the path, you'll find a very short descent over rocks to the waterline. A few brick steps have been built into this transition between trail and foreshore, but it's not really necessary, as the descent is neither steep nor challenging. There is no actual beach here; the rocks just gently descend into the shallows.

Tips

If you are interested in exploring Thompson Cove, there is a relatively new access trail that begins at the small car park located at the dogleg where Mount Newton Cross Road becomes Senanus Drive. The trail descends via a moderately steep set of stairs through the forest and deposits you at a small beach at the head of the cove.

10 DYER ROCKS

A little gem of a spot on the northern shore of Coles Bay, the Dyer Rocks are just off the tip of Yarrow Point. You are highly likely to have this spot to yourself: I rarely see beachgoers, picnickers or dog walkers here, and the limited walkable shoreline means it is not a great place to come for a stroll. But it is a lovely spot for a dip! Although the shoreline is forested, the trees are not tall, and the southwest-facing aspect means that both the beach and the rocks enjoy sunshine through most of the day.

The foreshore is characterized by a granite rock shelf that slopes out to sandy patches, dotted with eelgrass beds in the shallow intertidal zone. Even as you step into the water, you are likely to see leather and ochre stars, which are incredibly abundant here. Immediately to your left is a small cove, which is a mix of sand, rock and eelgrass where moon snails are common. Complete the circuit of this little bay—at its southern tip the rock is a bit steeper, often harbouring clusters of ochre stars as well as short plumose anemones.

However, the most interesting snorkelling is at the small islets, known as the Dyer Rocks, 100 metres or so offshore to your left from the trailhead. The lack of strong currents and boat traffic makes this an easy swim, even for beginners, and you should take your time studying the shallow bottom as you go. The rocky sides of the Dyer Rocks stay exposed and vegetation-free throughout the summertime, making for fine exploring year-round. You'll find clusters of large purple ochre stars and walls of delicate pink lightbulb tunicates. Sometimes sloping gently, but also with a few nice (shallow) vertical sections, the exposed rock here is rarely deeper than 4–5 metres. Farther away from the islets, at greater depths, the sea floor is actually quite barren, so the Dyer Rocks lend themselves to shallow exploration. Small fish species are quite abundant here, and on a sunny, good visibility day, you can almost convince yourself you are in the tropics (well, maybe). Coupled with the minimal currents and mostly shallow depths, the Dyer Rocks are an excellent place to bring beginners.

Lightbulb tunicates are a common sight in the Saanich Inlet.

Signature species

Lightbulb tunicates are present here in large numbers, forming bouquets of social colonies on rocks in the shallows. Gunnels are very common at Dyer Rocks, and I often see crowds of them slithering around the crabs and sea stars. Moon snails are also a frequent sight; the best place to search them out is in the little sandy cove just to the left of the main entry area. I often notice harbour seals here.

Critter list

Leather star, ochre star, mottled star, giant California sea cucumber, orange sea cucumber, pale sea cucumber, Monterey dorid, Hudson's dorid, clown nudibranch, lightbulb tunicate, shiny sea squirt, Lewis's moon snail, short plumose anemone, fried egg jelly, moon jelly, winged sea slug, squid eggs, gaper clam, red rock crab, crescent gunnel, penpoint gunnel.

Access

Approaching from West Saanich Road, turn onto Ardmore Drive (by the side of the golf course). Ardmore Drive ends in a T-junction; turn left (very confusingly, onto Ardmore Drive!) and continue just about 100 metres to a beach access on your right. Look for the white and red fire hydrant and small beach access sign, with a dirt pullout that is big enough for about four cars. The short (less than 100-metre), well-maintained gravel path takes you through a wooded area between houses and onto a granite rock shoreline. At high tide, this shallow foreshore is entirely submerged, all the way up to the trailhead. If entering at low tide, you'll be walking across the granite shelf. The swim from the entry point out to the Dyer Rocks is about 200 metres.

Tips

Since the snorkelling here is fairly shallow (no major fin propulsion required), and the entry is rocky, I usually come in my hard-soled booties and short plastic scuba fins. The vegetation stays fairly low here through the summer and is certainly no impediment to enjoying the abundant sea stars. The main nemesis of inlet snorkelling is the visibility, which can be highly variable (usually best in the fall).

SETCHELL POINT

11

At the south end of Deep Cove, Setchell Point is well known among the scuba community as the access point to a wreck dive in the bay. Although the wreck dive is not really a practical option for snorkellers, the shoreline of Deep Cove makes for a fine shallow destination. There is no beach here, just a set of stairs down to a narrow, rocky foreshore. Heading out to the right from the entry point offers some appealing terrain, including short vertical sections, boulders and small overhangs. Despite the steep sides, the depth is only about 5 metres at low tide, so you can explore the shallow subtidal zone without having to venture far from the shore. In addition to the natural coastline, there are numerous floats and pilings to explore, as well as a few underwater bits of scrap metal and dock chains. Much of this man-made terrain is coated with marine life, mostly mussels and short plumose anemones.

Along the rock walls, the piles of ochre stars will surely draw your eye, but there are plentiful diminutive delights here too. Much of the shallow subtidal rock is splattered with compound tunicate patches in shades of pastel peach and pink; shiny sea squirts hide in cracks, and yellow margin dorids are common. Fish are also quite plentiful here—keep your eyes open for brightly coloured painted greenling, one of the most attractive fish that inhabit the intertidal zone. Conversely, heading out left from the entry point is a bit duller—a more gradually sloping rock and sand bottom, and less wildlife.

These three yellow nudibranchs can be confusing for the beginner. The Monterey dorid (left) has black/brown tips on some of its tubercles. Heath's dorid (bottom left) has dark freckles on its main body, whose shape is flatter than the Monterey and often looks a bit ragged around the edges. The noble sea lemon (bottom right) is usually the largest of the three, with more extended dark patches on its body (but not on the tubercles) and a pale (often white) branchial plume.

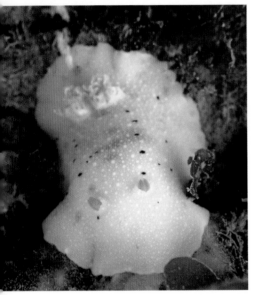

Critter list

Ochre star, leather star, mottled star, giant pink star, orange sea cucumber, pale sea cucumber, giant California sea cucumber, short plumose anemone, green urchin, fried egg jelly, shiny sea squirt, lined compound tunicate, giant rock scallop, black leather chiton, pile perch, blackeye goby, Pacific herring, painted greenling, copper rockfish, Monterey dorid, yellow margin dorid, Hudson's dorid.

Access

Setchell Road is a narrow residential street in the upmarket neighbourhood of Deep Cove. There is a small turnaround at the end of the road, and room for a handful of cars to park along the grass verge. A short set of a dozen or so stairs leads down to a bench that looks out north across the cove. The shoreline is accessed by a further (very short) dirt path down to the rocks, whence you can pick your entry point.

Tips

It's fairly shallow here, so timing with low tide is not particularly critical. The rocks and docks to the right of the entry point, which offer the best snorkelling terrain, are not much affected by summer vegetation. However, as with all inlet locales, the visibility can be pretty dodgy until late August, when clearer water days start to reappear.

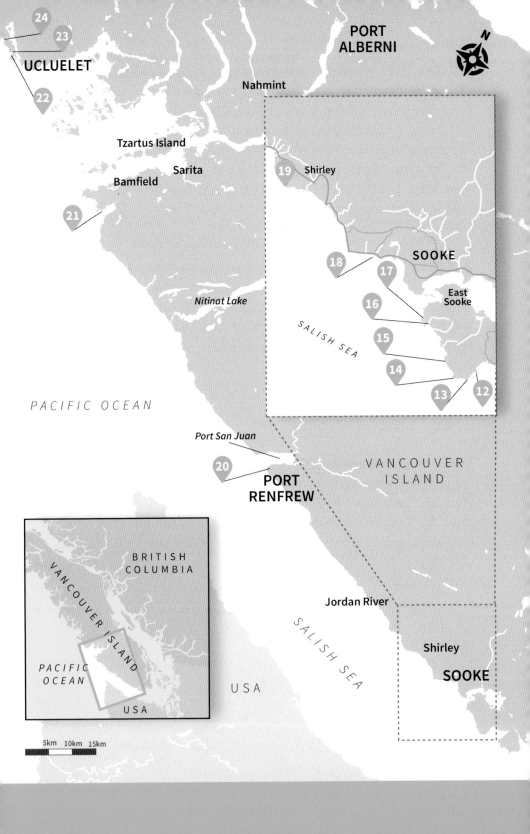

UCLUELET

24

23

22

PORT
ALBERNI

Nahmint

Tzartus Island

Sarita

Bamfield

21

Nitinat Lake

Shirley

19

18

17

16

SOOKE

East
Sooke

15

SALISH SEA

14

13

12

PACIFIC OCEAN

Port San Juan

20

PORT
RENFREW

VANCOUVER
ISLAND

Jordan River

SALISH SEA

Shirley

SOOKE

BRITISH
COLUMBIA

VANCOUVER ISLAND

PACIFIC
OCEAN

USA

USA

5km 10km 15km

THE WEST COAST

12

AYLARD FARM at EAST SOOKE PARK

Aylard Farm, and the snorkel out to Creyke Point, is one of the most accessible locations in East Sooke; consequently, it is also one of the busier spots in the region. The beach itself is wide and sandy, giving out onto a shallow bay, popular with families in the summertime. Indeed, many visitors venture no farther than this sandy strip, just a few hundred metres from the car park. Aylard Farm is also the most popular starting point for the numerous hikes within the regional park, whose number and variety provide something for every fitness level.

The snorkelling terrain at Aylard Farm is less wild (in terms of depth and exposure) than the other East Sooke Park locations in this guide, and consequently the wildlife is less high-octane. However, this is still a highly recommended spot, particularly for beginners, who will be wowed by the colourful critters in relatively shallow water. The east-facing aspect of the Aylard Farm beach means that it is also a little more protected from western winds and swell that washes relentlessly up the Juan de Fuca Strait.

Start your snorkel excursion by heading out left from the beach, where there are lots of rock shelves and blocky boulders to explore (heading out toward the right offers blander topography and less wildlife). For those comfortable with shallow diving, depths of just a few metres will allow you to check out numerous undercuts and overhangs, which almost always reveal some treasures. As you approach Creyke Point, there is a nice (although fairly short) cliff section, which provides some good diving opportunities. Be cautious as you reach the point, as the current may start to pick up here—you can poke your nose around the corner (there is a small beach here), but you will not be missing out on much additional terrain if you turn back now.

Signature species

Sunflower stars, which are more abundant here than I have seen elsewhere on the South Island, can be found in variety of colours from vivid orange to red and blue. As is the case for most of the East Sooke coastline, there is also an abundance of big rose anemones at depths that do not require any diving (as long as you haven't come at high tide).

Critter list

Sunflower star, striped sunstar, leather star, ochre star, mottled star, blood star, armpit blood star, vermilion star, drab six-armed star, short plumose anemone, giant plumose anemone, pink-tipped aggregating anemone, rose anemone, white-spotted rose anemone, stubby rose anemone, brooding anemone, white berthella, Monterey dorid, yellow margin dorid, frosted nudibranch, leopard dorid, San Diego dorid, clown nudibranch, giant white dorid, giant California sea cucumber, fried egg jelly, water jelly, lion's mane jelly, northern feather duster worm, giant Pacific chiton, hermit crab sponge.

Access

Parking for this location is at the main Aylard Farm lot in the regional park. On summer weekends this can get very busy, and unless you are arriving in the early half of the morning, you will likely have to park back on the road. Once you're parked, it is a few hundred metres' walk from the lot to the beach along a flat, well-trod trail and down a few steps at the end.

Sunflower stars in two of their many shades.

Tips

Even at relatively high tide, there is lots to see within the top few metres, making this a good winter destination (when the low tides are typically at night). The visibility is often poor at the beach itself, as a result of even the slightest wave action churning up the fine sand. But do not be discouraged—once you swim away from the beach, the visibility usually improves dramatically.

PETROGLYPHS at EAST SOOKE PARK

About a kilometre south of Aylard Farm, the petroglyphs are the first major landmark on East Sooke Park's Coast Trail. The dark rocks at the water's edge are etched with images made by the Coast Salish peoples and are estimated to be anywhere from a few hundred to three thousand years old. Looking out to sea from the petroglyphs, beyond a rich band of kelp, you'll see several small islets a few dozen metres offshore. This kelp line, which extends out about 50 metres from the shore, hugs the coast in both directions and lingers throughout the summer, into mid-fall.

The underwater terrain here offers lots of options. Immediately along the shoreline, on the inside of the kelp beds, there are clusters of northern feather duster worms enjoying the surf, along with armies of chitons, plentiful sea cucumbers and colonies of aggregating anemones. The area between the shore and the islets is fairly shallow, about 5 metres or so, and in the summer the bottom is fairly covered with leafy vegetation. Although this underwater foliage makes finding invertebrates on the rock surfaces hard work, this is great terrain for searching out colourful rock greenling. If the current is benign, swimming just outside the islets takes you quickly beyond the kelp beds to an exposed rocky bottom with some deeper diving opportunities. Alternatively, rather than heading directly out from shore, you can swim west (toward your right from the shore) to where the shoreline generates a gentle concave toward the north, making a bit of a bay. Cutting directly across this bay toward what look like cliffs (but which are actually quite shallow formations underwater) takes you across terrain that is about 10–15 metres deep, depending on the tide, where you'll find lots of goodies if you are comfortable exploring these depths.

Signature species

Lots of greenling lurk about in the shallows, often sitting quite still on their rock perches. If you are lucky, you will find an outrageously coloured rock greenling. On the sea star front, there are lots of northern sunstars here (the only other site at which I frequently see these is Iron Mine Bay).

Critter list

Rose anemone, white-spotted rose anemone, painted anemone, stubby rose anemone, green surf anemone, short plumose anemone, giant plumose anemone, pink-tipped aggregating anemone, brooding anemone, northern sunstar, sunflower star, striped sunstar, ochre star, leather star, mottled star, rainbow star, blood star, spiny red star, gooseneck barnacle, northern abalone, giant rock scallop, Puget Sound king crab, black leather chiton, giant Pacific chiton, lingcod, kelp greenling, rock greenling, pile perch, Pacific herring, black rockfish, orange sea cucumber, giant California sea cucumber, pale sea cucumber, armoured sea cucumber, red urchin, purple urchin, green urchin, hooded nudibranch, noble sea lemon, Monterey dorid, yellow margin dorid, orange cup coral, oval anchored stalk jelly, moon jelly, fried egg jelly, mauve lobed tunicate, orange social tunicate, northern feather duster worm.

Access

Park at the Aylard Farm lot. From here, there are two trail options to arrive at the petroglyphs: the Coast Trail and the Inland Trail, both approximately a kilometre from the parking lot. While the

Coast Trail is more scenic, it is fairly narrow and can get busy with hikers. It is also a bit more technical, with some rocky and rooty sections to pick your way over, and hence is overall a bit slower. Alternatively, the Inland Trail cuts across the grassy meadow to the south of the parking lot, and then into the forest. It is wide and well graded and much less frequented than the coastal option. A well-marked side trail to the left takes you to the petroglyphs.

Northern sunstar.

Once you're at the petroglyphs, there are several options for water entry. Take your pick from either entering directly below the carvings or walking a little further round the coast to make use of one of the numerous rock gullies that cut down to the water.

Tips

Boat traffic and strong currents are the major hazards to be aware of. There are also big sea lions patrolling these waters; in contrast to harbour seals, sea lions are quite confident in their interactions with divers, and become more so the longer you remain in the area. Be sure to follow marine regulations and retreat before they become emboldened to the point of nipping at your fins and fingers.

14

BEECHEY HEAD at EAST SOOKE PARK

Lying farther along East Sooke Park's Coast Trail from the petroglyphs, Beechey Head is another popular day hike from Aylard Farm. Hikers will be treated to a forested coastal path that provides shady walking and stunning vistas across the straits to the Olympic Mountains in the US. At Beechey Head itself, you can take a short scramble to the top of the lookout, whose cliffs drop down steeply to scattered boulders below. This is a favourite shoreline fishing spot for sure-footed anglers, who manage to navigate their way down to the shoreline to cast their lines into the salmon-rich waters. Descending with snorkel gear requires equal tenacity.

The snorkelling at Beechey Head, which marks the exposed southern tip of East Sooke, is not for the beginner. First, there is the hike in. This sounds deceptively easy—a mere 2 kilometres from the Aylard Farm parking lot, along a shady forest path (there is a shortcut through the inland area of the park, so you don't have to follow the Coast Trail). But factor in that you'll be

Northern staghorn bryozoan.

carrying all your gear (curse those lead weights!), that the terrain is deceptively hilly and that the scramble down to the water access is only for those descended from mountain goats, and the result is a fairly high-energy destination. Even if you have some hardy friends who scoff at the prospect of lugging lead, the currents here can pick up quickly. There is also significant boat traffic that can be unnerving, as well as exposure to the open ocean (next stop: the Olympics), but for those up for the challenge, this is another highly rewarding East Sooke location with an excellent diversity of species and interesting underwater terrain.

Underwater, the cliffs drop off fairly steeply, but with ledges and overhangs that are fun for the more advanced snorkeller to explore. That said, the wildlife and topography here are quite similar to Iron Mine Bay, which offers considerably easier access. In the summertime, there is a reasonable amount of kelp, and it is delightful to glide through the fronds with the glittering shoals of silver fish. However, the rocks themselves are exposed, making Beechey Head a good summer destination when most of the south coast is hiding beneath an underwater jungle.

Signature species

The most satisfying wildlife experience here is encountering the numerous compound tunicate colonies, particularly the mauve lobed variety, which look like big purple sponges. There is also a good variety of sea stars here, with striped sunstars and spiny red stars being particularly common. As with many East Sooke locations, there is a good selection of anemones, including a decent-sized colony of giant plumose anemones, and even a couple of crimsons.

Critter list

Rose anemone, white-spotted rose anemone, stubby rose anemone, crimson anemone, giant plumose anemone, painted anemone, green surf anemone, noble sea lemon, Monterey dorid, yellow margin dorid, giant Pacific chiton, black leather chiton, red urchin, purple urchin, green urchin, giant California sea cucumber, orange sea cucumber, armoured sea cucumber, striped sunstar, rainbow star, spiny red star, ochre star, leather star, blood star, armpit blood star, mauve lobed tunicate, giant Pacific octopus.

Access

Park at Aylard Farm and hike approximately 2 kilometres to Beechey Head along the inland forest trail. Once you're at Beechey Head, the easiest water access is to head left (east) when you hit the Coast Trail; walk approximately 100 metres along this path and you will see a sloping access down to the rocky shoreline. Once you're at the shoreline, it's a matter of picking a friendly-looking entry point, which will be tide-dependent. The rocks are heavily barnacled, so bring your beater fins and booties and save your fancy carbon-fibre mermaid accessories for another day. It is also possible to scramble down the rocks right at the headland itself (presumably this is what the fisherfolk do), but this always looks a bit precarious for my taste.

Tips

Beware the very strong currents that rip along this coastline, and the back eddies that mean that the water direction is often counterintuitive. If you are wearing hard-soled booties, you can always treat this as a drift snorkel—let the current carry you along the coastline as far as you feel comfortable and then hike back (though it is not the entire coastline that lends itself to water egress and trail access, so keep an eye on the beach conditions).

The waters off Beechey Head boast some of the best salmon fishing grounds in the South Island. Although the boats tend to stay offshore, keep an eye out for potential fast flybys and wakes.

CABIN POINT at EAST SOOKE PARK

15

Another 2 kilometres along the Coast Trail from Beechey Head is Cabin Point, marking the approximate halfway point between Aylard Farm and Iron Mine Bay. Just before Cabin Point (if you're approaching from Beechey Head), the trail drops naturally down to a wonderful pocket beach with a vista out through two narrow channels. These channels are actually the two sides of a small island that connects with the main coast at low tides (indeed, on many maps it is shown as a continuation of the Vancouver Island coastline). The beach itself is composed of small smooth pebbles, with some pleasant driftwood to mooch around on. Owing to its proximity to one of East Sooke Park's most popular trails (the Coast Trail), there can be a surprising amount of hiker traffic here on fine summer days, but if you come out of season, you will almost certainly have the place to yourself.

As with most East Sooke snorkel locations (the beach at Aylard Farm being the main exception), Cabin Point is very exposed to current and swell. Although this demands respect for the local conditions and a careful eye on the tide tables, the reward for the snorkeller is a vital underwater landscape characterized by super-sized anemones and colourful sea stars. However, novices (or those who simply failed to consult the current prediction in advance) can stay in the relatively protected channels and will likely still have a fine old time.

The channel leading out from the right-hand side of the beach is narrow and shallow, such that at low tide in the summertime, it can be challenging to navigate over both terrain

Lingcod.

and foliage. Better, in my humble snorkelling opinion, is to strike out from the channel on the left of the beach. The rocky side of the "island" has interesting mini-critters from the get-go, and you will find little clusters of short plumose anemones, chitons and six-armed stars. In the summertime, the shallow bottom of the channel is fairly covered in vegetation, but once you ease your way through the splendid kelp forest toward the southern point, you will have plenty of exposed rock to explore. The underwater terrain is quite steep—on a good visibility day, you can peer down and spot large anemones, urchins and sea stars on the plummeting rock face.

Critter list

Sunflower star, striped sunstar, rainbow star, drab six-armed star, ochre star, leather star, spiny red star, blood star, short plumose anemone, giant plumose anemone, pink-tipped aggregating anemone, green surf anemone, brooding anemone, painted anemone, rose anemone, white-spotted rose anemone, mushroom compound tunicate, mauve lobed tunicate, orange cup coral, orange sea cucumber, giant California sea cucumber, armoured sea cucumber, pale sea cucumber, noble sea lemon, green urchin, red urchin, purple urchin, Puget Sound king crab, giant Pacific chiton, mossy chiton, black leather chiton, lined chiton, fried egg jelly, northern feather duster worm.

Access

East Sooke Park's Coast Trail naturally skirts the beach access for this location; if you are coming from Beechey Head and you hit Cabin Point, you have gone just a bit too far. The total hiking distance from the Aylard Farm parking lot to Cabin Point is anywhere between 3 kilometres (if you take the inland route) and almost 5 kilometres (if you take the Coast Trail the whole way). The hybrid option is to take the inland route to Beechey Head (2 kilometres) and then follow the Coast Trail the final 2 kilometres. These distances might not sound large, but if you have any previous experience lugging your snorkel gear more than a few hundred metres, you will know to treat this approach with respect!

Much more enjoyable is to arrive by boat. Although the distance from Aylard Farm (the closest easy launch point) is eminently manageable for recreational kayakers, the often wild conditions (read: swell and current) mean that this is no small undertaking. It is a challenge to find a window of low current long enough to make the paddle out, snorkel and then paddle back. So, in practice, Cabin Point is most easily visited by motorized craft, ideally one that is small enough to anchor in the bay of the channel leading up to the beach. This anchorage is very sheltered, and the shallow pebble beach means that small craft can be readily hauled above the tide line.

Tips

Find a friend with a boat. The Cheanuh Marina at Spirit Bay is the most obvious launch spot, with Pedder Bay as an alternative option, a little farther along the coast.

16

IRON MINE BAY at EAST SOOKE PARK

Iron Mine Bay is a lovely little pebble and sand bay accessed by a short (five-minute) forest trail in East Sooke Park, and one of my all-time favourite snorkel locations on Vancouver Island. Arguably, the prime real estate at Iron Mine Bay is the cliffs that you can reach by heading out to the right from the main beach. There are abundant and varied species and interesting topography at a nice range of depths for the snorkeller (with a maximum of about 10 metres). The far south-facing tip (Pike Point) is one of the highlights of this section for the more accomplished diver, as the walls drop off vertically for farther than I can see (or dive), making this a good place to explore the subtidal zone.

On your immediate left from the beach is a small, rocky peninsula that is particularly good for beginners, thanks to its proximity to the shore and abundance of underwater riches. Even in this limited area, I have seen a variety of sea stars and nudibranchs, and there are numerous resident rose anemones. However, the shallows in this section are covered with vegetation from late spring to late summer.

Following the coastline to the left of the beach for a few hundred metres, you will reach another rocky promontory (which turns into an island at low tide). The underwater terrain here is quite striking and offers some deeper diving options. I saw my first orange peel nudibranch here—a rare sighting for the snorkeller, as this species is predominantly subtidal.

Signature species

All sorts of great sea stars! Northern sunstars, which I rarely see anywhere else on the island, are quite plentiful here. Striped sunstars are also common. Rainbow stars seem to love the East Sooke coastline, and you'll almost certainly see them in abundance here. And I have also spotted several of the lesser-seen species here, such as a velcro star, spiny red star and giant pink star (all at the southern tip of Pike Point). As with much of the Sooke coastline, you will also be treated to numerous large rose anemones. In late September/early October, look for hooded nudibranchs on the kelp fronds.

Spiny red star.

Critter list

Striped sunstar, cushion star, ochre star, spiny red star, velcro star, drab six-armed star, giant pink star, leather star, northern sunstar, rainbow star, sunflower star, blood star, red urchin, purple urchin, green urchin, painted anemone, rose anemone, white-spotted rose anemone, green surf anemone, brooding anemone, short plumose anemone, giant plumose anemone, noble sea lemon, orange peel nudibranch, Monterey dorid, Hudson's dorid, Heath's dorid, white berthella, three-lined aeolid, yellow margin dorid, giant white dorid, leopard dorid, hooded nudibranch, northern feather duster worm, giant California sea cucumber, orange sea cucumber, armoured sea cucumber, pale sea cucumber, lined chiton, black leather chiton, giant Pacific chiton, fried egg jelly, winged sea slug, comb jelly, northern staghorn bryozoan, Puget Sound king crab, giant acorn barnacle.

Access

To make the walk-in as short as possible, don't park in the regular East Sooke Park lot. Instead, head toward the end of Silver Spray Drive and park just outside the resort gates in the wide turning area. On foot, proceed through the first gate and take the first left. Technically, this is Ocean Park Place, but at the time of writing it was no more than a dirt drive with a few trailers at the end. Although ongoing development makes description of the access here particularly subject to change, the trail at the end of Ocean Park Place is part of East Sooke Park (Silver Spray Trail), so public access should be protected from private development. The trail through the forest down to the beach takes about five minutes and the turning off to the right for Iron Mine Bay is well signposted.

Tips

I like to visit Iron Mine Bay in the morning so that I can enjoy the sun on the cliff wall (though this location is quite prone to morning mists).

Although the east-facing cliffs offer protection from the Juan de Fuca swell and prevailing wind direction, Pike Point sticks its nose right out into the open ocean and can be pounded if the swell is up.

★ SILVER SPRAY BEACH and POSSESSION POINT

17

A little gem of a beach in East Sooke, just outside the regional park's boundaries, with lots of real estate to explore. The beach itself is pebbly, giving out into a sandy bay underwater. The western swell that comes down the Strait of Juan de Fuca means that there is often significant wave action here, so you have to time your visit to coincide with calmer waters. The benefit of this constant exposure to swell is that it emulates a high-current environment, and there are consequently surge-loving species such as abundant (and large) white-spotted rose anemones, and also a good population of green surf anemones. However, high current is very much a reality toward the southern tip of Possession Point, where the SookePoint Ocean Cottage resort teeters above you on the cliffs.

Heading out from the right-hand side of the beach offers some nicely varied terrain, including cliffs, undercuts and even some boulder tunnels to swim through if the tide allows. There are several rocky reefs exposed at low tide that are covered in huge mussel colonies, as well as the usual intertidal carpets of barnacles and aggregating

White-spotted rose anemone.

anemones. The obvious "cliff" has a compact collection of giant plumose anemones just a few metres below the surface, under a shallow overhang. All of this terrain is relatively shallow, so on a calm day this is a great spot for beginners. The wildlife is instantly rewarding too—lots of big ochre and mottled stars in a variety of hues, and plentiful oversized anemones in colours from ruby red to lime green.

Heading out left from the beach, it is about 450 metres to the far end of the peninsula (Possession Point), and exploring all the little nooks and crannies along the way makes for a fairly full excursion. The first half of the swim out to the point is largely protected from current, but in the summertime this stretch is covered in leafy vegetation. Consequently, if you visit between April and September, you will want to strike out toward the point where the rock remains exposed, thanks to the more vertical real estate and higher current exposure. Indeed, the water here seems to be always on the move, and in ways that seem to defy prediction. I only ever entertain the idea of rounding the point when the tide is close to slack, and I regularly check that I am still able to swim against it. However, if conditions permit this approach, you may be lucky enough to find one of several patches of strawberry anemones. If you have any stamina left after the long swim and any current battles, it is worthwhile to poke your way around the point and through the narrow channel that is formed by a small offshore islet. The walls here are steep and deep, and you'll find numerous clusters of giant plumose anemones (particularly on the north wall of the islet).

Signature species

Rose anemones, and particularly white-spotted rose anemones, are more abundant here than I have seen anywhere else. Stubby rose anemones abound, particularly on the right-hand side from the beach (green surf anemones are also plentiful in this direction). There are several clusters of strawberry anemones close to the tip of Possession Point, as well as colonies of giant plumose anemones, with the largest groups located on the north wall of the islet. The orange cup corals are also very lovely here.

Critter list

Rose anemone, white-spotted rose anemone, stubby rose anemone, short plumose anemone, giant plumose anemone, strawberry anemone, green surf anemone, pink-tipped aggregating anemone, giant California sea cucumber, orange sea cucumber, armoured sea cucumber, green urchin, red urchin, purple urchin, mottled star, blood star, spiny red star, sunflower star, giant pink star, striped sunstar, armpit blood star, rainbow star, vermilion star, leather star, noble sea lemon, Monterey dorid, leopard dorid, yellow margin dorid, Nanaimo dorid, buffalo sculpin, kelp greenling, orange cup coral, giant Pacific chiton, black leather chiton, mauve lobed tunicate, northern feather duster worm, moon jelly.

Access

As for Iron Mine Bay, park just outside the gates of the resort. The access to Silver Spray Beach is quite well concealed, cutting between two private properties (look for house number 1130) about 100 metres back along Silver Spray Drive from the pullout parking. The trail is quite short (around 70 metres), but steep.

Tips

This is typically not a winter destination, owing to the relentless Juan de Fuca swell that generates significant waves, degrades visibility and is rarely calm during the winter months. But never fear: if the swell looks a bit iffy, you have not had a wasted drive. The cliffs at Iron Mine Bay are east-facing, so are usually calmer.

18 OTTER POINT ISLETS (Sooke)

Otter Point Resort is the rather euphemistically named trailer park located about 7 kilometres beyond Sooke, on Highway 14. The resort enjoys several hundred metres of prime beachfront real estate that looks out over the Juan de Fuca Strait. Since the resort itself is emphatically private, and bordered on both sides by private residential lots, to the casual passerby there appears no option for public beach access here. However, there is a well-disguised public easement shown on the Otter Point zoning map that is immediately to the east of the trailer park; see the "Access" section below for more details.

About 100 metres offshore from the beach is a cluster of islets, the tops of which are exposed even during the highest of tides. There is also a smaller, shallow reef slightly to the east of the islets and close to shore, marked by a rocky outcrop that extends all the way to the pebble beach. I like to visit these beachside reefs on my way out to the islets; despite their shallower setting, there is a pleasant variety of intertidal life to explore. As long as the current isn't running up a storm (see "Tips" below), it is then a short and easy swim across to the islets; the water in the interim is not deep, and on a good visibility day you will be able to see the bottom the entire way.

The terrain at the islets is ideal for the snorkeller, with rocky sides that drop down to depths of no more than 5–10 metres, depending on the tide height. Those who stick to the shallows can explore the fields of oversized California mussels and tricolour urchins. In the intertidal saddles between the islets, there are substantial bouquets of northern feather duster worms emerging from foot-long tubes to catch the passing buffet. Although nudibranchs are thin on the ground, the variety of sea stars here is excellent, and I have spotted several of my favourite species (including cushion, striped and sunflower) here. Those who can dive to explore under the overhangs will be rewarded with ceilings of orange zoanthids and peach-coloured lobed compound tunicates, providing plenty of colour.

Cushion (slime) star.

Critter list

Red urchin, purple urchin, green urchin, ochre star, leather star, mottled star, sunflower star, striped sunstar, rainbow star, cushion star, blood star, drab six-armed star, colourful six-armed star, northern feather duster worm, lobed compound tunicate, black leather chiton, kelp greenling, blackeye goby, painted anemone, rose anemone, short plumose anemone, giant plumose anemone, green surf anemone, brooding anemone, giant California sea cucumber, orange sea cucumber, armoured sea cucumber, giant acorn barnacle, orange cup coral, California mussel, comb jelly, orange zoanthid, hooded nudibranch, cross jelly.

Access

Park at the pullout in front of the mailboxes on the eastern side of Otter Point Resort, where Carpenter Road joins West Coast

Road (Highway 14) from the north. There is room for just a few cars here, but you are unlikely to have much company (unless there's a sudden rush on flyer deliveries). The public access to the beach is about 20 metres wide, and is located on the eastern side of the trailer park, running between the resort and house number 7863. From the highway, it looks like a private driveway; this drops down to a gravel track, with a grassy area on your right (eventually bordering the trailer park). The latter is my preferred approach, just to respect the privacy of the folks in the houses that border this track (and to avoid any uncomfortable discussions about zoning boundaries). From the highway to the beach is a mere 100 metres or so.

Tips

The current here can be significant, and predicting its strength (and even its direction) has defied all my attempts to find a correlation with various forecasts and charts. Suffice to say that I have resigned myself to simply turning up and seeing what the ocean gods have in store. The good news is that the current direction is lateral, so if the flow picks up while you are out at the islets, the most likely outcome is that you have a longer walk back to your gear dump.

In addition to the current, the main impediment to snorkelling here is the surf. Even on low wind days, the accumulated energy from the open Pacific can translate into a sizable onshore swell. Although there are numerous wave forecast websites and apps that cater to the surf crowd, there is no substitute for simply being able to look at the surface conditions. Fortunately, there are several websites that host webcam footage from Gordon's Beach, which is just a stone's throw from Otter Point, as well as Sheringham Point.

CHITONS

Chitons are an extremely numerous and diverse type of marine mollusc that is common in the intertidal zone. Even within a given species, colours can vary dramatically, as seen here with several examples of the lined chiton (bottom row and top left). The giant Pacific (gumboot) chiton (middle right) is usually a fairly drab pink but is the largest in the world and can weigh up to two kilograms! Also shown are the mossy chiton (top right) and black leather chiton (middle left).

19 SHERINGHAM POINT LIGHTHOUSE

Built in 1912, the dramatic 20-metre-high structure of Sheringham Point Lighthouse is located in the community of Shirley, some 60 kilometres from Victoria. The need for a shipping beacon is a dead giveaway that this is a particularly gnarly piece of the Sooke coastline, not only prone to big waves but also home to craggy underwater reefs. Suffice to say that this is not an easy stretch of coastline for the snorkeller. It is exposed to wind, waves and swell, experiences strong currents and has a steep, rocky topography that is not for the faint of heart. Swimming here requires waiting for good conditions, which are not always predictable, and completely flat water is a rarity. Fortunately, a visit here is never a wasted journey, as the small trail network is delightful, the view of and from the lighthouse is stunning (although entry inside is not permitted), and the Shirley Delicious Café is close at hand for sweet treats and fine caffeinated beverages.

The main snorkelling areas are the bays to the left and right of the point. If there is light wind or swell, you will likely be able to find some shelter on at least one of the two sides (anything more than "light" and you should stay dry and come back another day). I find the bay to the left (east) to be more rewarding in terms of both underwater terrain and wildlife: lots of reefs, colourful life on the rocks and a beautiful kelp forest. The bay to the right also has some nice underwater features but is less dramatic. It also seems to have succumbed to a purple urchin infestation that has mown the majority of the kelp, and generally has less abundant and varied wildlife and colour.

Signature species

Considering that sunflower stars are officially listed as critically endangered, they are frequently sighted here. Indeed, on my first visit to Sheringham Point I think I saw more sunflower stars (half a dozen or so) than any other sea star species.

Critter list

Rose anemone, white-spotted rose anemone, stubby rose anemone, green surf anemone, painted anemone, brooding anemone, giant California sea cucumber, black leather chiton, giant Pacific chiton, lined chiton, kelp greenling, leopard dorid, Monterey dorid, yellow margin dorid, noble sea lemon, striped sunstar, rainbow star, sunflower star, leather star, blood star, armpit blood star, drab six-armed star, moon jelly, cross jelly, shiny sea squirt, gooseneck barnacle, California mussel, red Pacific octopus, red urchin, green urchin, purple urchin.

Kelp crabs are one of the most common crustacean species you'll see while snorkelling. This one is sporting a jaunty brooding-anemone cap.

Access

The turnoff for the lighthouse (Sheringham Point Road) is signposted from West Coast Road (Highway 14) and is on your left as you drive from Victoria or Sooke. Look out for the Shirley Delicious Café at the junction. Follow Sheringham Point Road for about a kilometre and a half, until it comes to an end in a small car park. From here, there is a well-marked, well-graded gravel trail through the forest. Follow the trail for about 200 metres before it pops out onto a road; cross the road and enter the gate (open to pedestrians but not vehicles) to the lighthouse property. The opening hours of the gate change with the season; check the website for the current schedule before you go (sheringhamlighthouse .org). From the gate, it is about another 300 metres down a winding gravel road.

The lighthouse stands at the end of a small, rocky promontory. Steep, craggy rocks descend on both the left and the right, with scary-looking signs showing people falling off cliffs and declarations of no access. At the tip of the point, the signs merely indicate that you continue at your own risk. Continue at your own risk. I find that the easiest entry is at the very (southern) tip of the point, where the smooth volcanic rock is steep, but readily navigated.

Tips

Water entry here can be decidedly tricky. The rocks are steep and covered with mussels and barnacles below the high-tide mark. Since the depth of the two bays is only about 4–7 metres, slack high is a good time to come, combining easier water entry and low currents, without compromising the accessible terrain.

There are very thick kelp beds here in the summer. If you're visiting between May and September, your movements will be somewhat hampered by the dense growth. The kelp has usually thinned out sufficiently by late October, making fall the ideal time to visit (before the winter storms and swell start to gain in energy).

BOTANY BAY (Juan de Fuca Provincial Park)

Botany Bay is located at the north end of Botanical Beach, close to Port Renfrew. Originally an independent provincial park, Botanical Beach was combined with two other existing parks (Loss Creek and China Beach) to form Juan de Fuca Provincial Park in 1996. The resulting mega-park includes previously unprotected areas covering Mystic Beach and Sombrio Beach. Today, Juan de Fuca Provincial Park is one of the most popular parks on the South Island, encompassing some 50 kilometres of contiguous coastline that boasts spectacular beaches and forest wilderness.

Botany Bay is the first stop along the northern end of the Juan de Fuca trailhead, less than a kilometre from the parking lot, just beyond Port Renfrew. After you descend through the forest, your vista opens to a fabulous pebble beach that has been chiselled into the surrounding granite coastline. Seams of glittering white quartz split the otherwise black rock, whose layers of volcanic slate are stacked in ancient angles. A tree-topped islet stands sentinel in the middle of the bay; to its right, the water is both very shallow and exposed to wave action. Consequently, the best area for snorkelling is to its left. It's not a large area, stretching no more than 100 metres from the shore to the outer rocks that protect the bay from the waves, and you may find your exploration space is truncated on days with higher surf.

Despite its modest extent, the underwater terrain here is nice and varied, with lots of boulders, slabs and overhangs, all in less than 10 metres of water. The marine wildlife is decent, though not as impressive as some of the other West Coast locations in

Stubby rose anemones.

this guide. The most common critters are purple urchins and various anemones. A small kelp grove forms in the middle of the bay in the summertime, and in addition to the invertebrate life there are plentiful greenling living in this little community. Despite the relatively understated wildlife showing, the combination of Botany Bay's spectacular setting and varied underwater terrain makes it fully deserving of a visit.

Signature species

Stubby rose anemones are abundant at Botany Bay, taking advantage of the shale sand bottom to bury themselves, often snuggled up against the rock boundary.

Critter list

Leather star, rainbow star, blood star, drab six-armed star, colourful six-armed star, purple urchin, red urchin, green urchin, stubby rose anemone, pink-tipped aggregating anemone, green surf anemone, white-spotted rose anemone, painted anemone, shiny sea squirt, orange cup coral, kelp greenling, lingcod, lined chiton, giant Pacific chiton, mossy chiton, giant white dorid, red sponge dorid, Monterey dorid, Heath's dorid, leopard dorid, white berthella, giant rock scallop, calcareous tube worm, orange sea cucumber, armoured sea cucumber, cross jelly, sharpnose crab.

Access

Arriving at Port Renfrew, follow the signs to Botanical Beach. The parking lot is located at the end of Cerantes Road. There is lots of parking space here, some picnic tables and several pit toilets at the trailhead. Follow the signs down to Botany Bay. It is about a 700-metre walk downhill along a wide, well-maintained trail. As you approach the coast, the trail splits—heading left will take you on toward the main part of Botanical Beach where the tide pools are. Veer to the right and you'll go down a few steps and emerge on the pebble beach of Botany Bay.

Tips

I have never seen the outer reef of Botany Bay without waves. Even on days when the surf zones at Jordan River have been like glass, there is still a wave party happening here. And I don't just mean a few breakers on the shore; I mean the pound-you-to-dust-on-the-rocks kind of waves. On relatively calm days, the bay itself is sufficiently protected for safe snorkelling. But it is inadvisable to extend your exploration into the open ocean.

Since the bay is relatively shallow (no deeper than 10 metres, even at the highest of tides), timing your visit with low tide is not critical. However, if you have family members planning to explore the tide pools along Botanical Beach, then a low tide will be important for them (the BC Parks website recommends a tide no higher than 1.2 metres, based on Port Renfrew tide tables).

21 PACHENA BAY ISLETS

Pachena Bay is an iconic sandy beach located along the Pacific Rim National Park Reserve and is a true West Coast beauty. The beach itself is almost a kilometre long, and at low tide the fine yellow sand extends a few hundred metres out from shore. From here, you can watch resident ospreys patrolling above the shallows, on the lookout for their next catch. Bald eagles, ravens, loons and pigeon guillemots count among the other avian wild-life attractions. You may even get lucky and be visited by whales, which have been known to come into the bay to feed.

The big, sandy beach is not at all interesting for snorkelling (but very fine for swimming and skim boarding). Instead, the best way to reach prime snorkelling territory is by kayak; the shallow, sandy beach offers easy launching, once you have waded out past the breakers. From the beach, you will see a rocky point (Clutus Point) at the end of the right-hand shoreline. Aim for this directly or pootle along the shoreline, as you wish. At the far end of the bay, just before Clutus Point, is a wide pebble beach, a short distance from which are several rocky islets—this is your snorkel destination. Beach your kayak and suit up!

The islets offer an ideal snorkel location—the depths are fairly shallow (no more than 5 metres, depending on the tide) and the reefs form a natural protective barrier from the incoming swell. In the summertime, the islets harbour forests of various kelp varieties: bull, giant and feather boa, which host a myriad of small fish and crabs among their fronds. Although the shallows have some vegetation, the modest covering of rockweed and

Pachena Bay was thick with thousands of red-eyed medusas during my first visit.

scattered clumps of dead man's fingers only add to the appeal. You will have no trouble spotting colourful invertebrates despite the summer foliage.

Signature species

Green surf anemones abound, and you'll see literally hundreds of ochre stars. Whereas the South Island hosts mostly the purple variety, here you will find the full spectrum of colours: orange, pink, brown and violet, all piled atop one another in massive orgies.

Critter list

Frosted nudibranch, Heath's dorid, Monterey dorid, leopard dorid, green surf anemone, painted anemone, white-spotted rose anemone, short plumose anemone, stubby rose anemone, pink-tipped aggregating anemone, black leather chiton, red-eyed medusa, fried egg jelly, orange sea cucumber, pale sea cucumber, ochre star, mottled star, leather star, sunflower star, lightbulb tunicate, compound mushroom tunicate, stalked tunicate, red urchin, purple urchin, orange cup coral, gooseneck barnacle.

Access

Access to Pachena Bay is via logging roads, either from Youbou (which is shorter, but you'll spend more time on gravel) or from Port Alberni. From the beach at Pachena Bay, it is about a 3-kilometre paddle to Clutus Point and its islets. The shortest swim crossing to the islands requires landing at the start of the stretch of beach that carves a wide crescent at the end of the peninsula. The beach itself is part of a pocket of First Nations land within the Pacific Rim National Park Reserve, but a sign at the beach indicates that respectful day use of the beach is permitted.

Tips

This is bear country! Having completed a little post-snorkel kayak exploration, we swung back past the beach where we had stationed ourselves for lunch, only to find a black bear sniffing around for leftovers. This was a good reminder not to leave food unattended on the beach while snorkelling—it would be suboptimal to return after your swim to find your tacos had been snaffled.

Camping at Pachena is popular on summer weekends and requires advance booking (there is an online reservation system that makes this a breeze). However, mid-week, as long as you are happy to take a forest spot (rather than prime beach real estate), you are fairly likely to be able to make a spur-of-the-moment decision to visit.

Assess conditions carefully before you head out. Pachena Bay's waters are fairly protected from strong currents, but they face the open ocean and are subject to a rolling swell even on calm days. Also be mindful of the wind forecast—coupling a southwester with the ocean swell can make for active seas.

TERRACE BEACH
(Ucluelet)

22

The coastline of the Ucluelet peninsula would make Slartibartfast swell with pride at all of its crinkly bits. The southern tip is particularly spectacular, with deeply notched black-rock cliffs, hollowed-out tide pools, and splintered islets. The treacherous nature of these fractal shores is alluded to by the presence of Amphitrite Point Lighthouse, located on a popular walking loop at the southern end of the Wild Pacific Trail. Against the backdrop of these wave-pounded shores, Terrace Beach offers an oasis of calm water, ideal snorkelling terrain and a wonderful wildlife show.

Terrace Beach is located adjacent to the Wild Pacific Trail lighthouse loop. Sheltered by two rocky headlands, the beach is set back in a naturally protected harbour, whose waters are further calmed by underwater reefs offshore. The bay itself is large, and there is a lot of real estate to explore; how far from the beach you wander may be limited by external wave conditions, as the chop and swell are likely to pick up the closer you approach the headlands. The middle of the bay is mostly just sand and fairly shallow; you won't find much here except for (lots of) moon snails. The most rewarding regions for critter spotting are along the rocky shorelines.

Although both sides of the bay offer a variety of marine wildlife to discover, my personal preference is for the shoreline off to the left-hand edge of the beach. There is a particularly nice rocky reef about 100 metres offshore (exposed at low tide) that I find hosts a reliably good critter selection. In this same direction, you can detour into a little channel that leads to a sandy

The San Diego dorid (top) and leopard dorid (bottom) may look similar, but they have been identified as distinct species.

beach (He-Tin-Kis Beach, also accessible via stairs from the lighthouse loop trail). At the end of the channel, your progress will likely be thwarted by surf and waves, but this little section is particularly good for green surf anemones.

Signature species

Bat stars (I only ever see these around the Ucluelet coastline and in Barkley Sound), moon snails (lots in the shallow, sandy middle area), and noble sea lemons (although a reasonably common species, I have never seen them in such abundance as at Terrace Beach).

Critter list

Green surf anemone, white-spotted rose anemone, rose anemone, painted anemone, pink-tipped aggregating anemone, short plumose anemone, leather star, ochre star, mottled star, bat star, giant white dorid, noble sea lemon, leopard dorid, San Diego dorid, Monterey dorid, frosted nudibranch, yellow margin dorid, red urchin, orange cup coral, Lewis's moon snail, lined chiton, giant California sea cucumber, shiny sea squirt.

Access

There are two options for parking and beach access. The first option is to use the parking lot attached to the Terrace Beach Resort. Although the lot is reasonably spacious (and designated for use by the public wanting access to the beach), it is often filled with cars belonging to resort guests. However, if you do manage to snag a spot here, the trail to the water is a mere 20 metres or so through the forest, and deposits you right in the middle of the beach. Alternatively, you can use the (also reasonably spacious) lot at the south end of Terrace Beach, located at He-Tin-Kis Park. This lot serves as one of the access points to the Wild Pacific Trail's popular lighthouse loop. From the He-Tin-Kis Park lot, the walk is along a gradually descending forest trail about 100 metres long.

Tips

Terrace Beach gets very vegetated in the summer. Since it is largely protected from the open ocean conditions, I have had good luck visiting here in the winter.

Several Ucluelet locations are covered by webcams that can be handy for checking conditions before you head out: www.ukeelivecams.com.

Don't miss the walking loop out to the lighthouse—it's a fabulous little trail with spectacular views of the coastline, pocket beaches and the lighthouse itself. There is also a pleasant little inland boardwalk loop that takes you through a boggy marsh, with interpretative signs identifying the species.

23

LITTLE BEACH (Ucluelet)

Little Beach is Terrace Beach's sibling, located just a stone's throw to the north. The two locations have an almost identical topographic layout: rocky shoreline, shallow intertidal reefs and a sandy midsection. Perhaps not surprisingly then, a very similar range of species is found at both beaches. However, Little Beach is (ironically) just a bit larger and a bit shallower than Terrace. I rate the latter a little higher, as I find it to have more interesting underwater architecture, but Little Beach is still a fine spot and well worth a visit.

The right-hand (northern) shore of Little Beach is particularly shallow, and you'll need to swim at least 100 metres from the entry to start to find interesting terrain. In contrast, the left-hand rim is immediately rewarding, with lots of green surf anemones in the intertidal zone. Indeed, at tides below about 1.5 metres, most of these anemones will actually be exposed above the waterline. The terrain gets more interesting, and the species more varied, the farther out you go. After some 400 metres, you will reach a small point; the coastline now turns back on itself and heads back in toward Terrace Beach.

Like Terrace Beach, the sandy bay of Little Beach is largely barren except for hoards of moon snails marauding across its shallows. There is a healthy growth of giant kelp throughout these shallows in the summertime, which can be a bit of a battle to navigate. Visiting in the fall offers a nice balance between shoreline accessibility and kelp viewing. Indeed, once the forest

Leather stars (left) and bat stars (right) have similar shapes, with webbing between their five (sometimes six) arms. However, whereas leather stars are common all around Vancouver Island and have a standard mottled pattern and colouration, bat stars are found on the exposed outer coast and are uniform in colour, with shades ranging from dark grey to bright orange.

has thinned back, the stipe real estate is in high demand by kelp crabs, and you'll find them duelling over territories.

Signature species

Ochre stars may be a common sight around Vancouver Island, but at Little Beach they are notable for their abundance, size and variety of colours. Armies of moon snails patrol the sandy shallows in search of clams.

Buffalo sculpins are so confident in their camouflage that you can often sneak quite close for a snapshot.

Critter list

Ochre star, bat star, armpit blood star, drab six-armed star, leather star, green surf anemone, short plumose anemone, pink-tipped aggregating anemone, giant rock scallop, orange cup coral, northern abalone, kelp greenling, lingcod, sharpnose crab, red urchin, Monterey dorid, leopard dorid, San Diego dorid, giant white dorid, frosted nudibranch, noble sea lemon, Nanaimo dorid, mushroom compound tunicate, Lewis's moon snail.

Access

The Little Beach parking lot is well signposted off Peninsula Road. Although there are only a handful of marked stalls, you could fit a dozen or so cars in here if you use the space to its full extent. The walk to the beach is mere steps.

Tips

No need to time your snorkel at Little Beach with the tide! The whole area is fairly shallow, with depths rarely exceeding 5 metres or so. Indeed, many of the green surf anemones will be exposed if you come at very low tides.

COOPER'S BEACH
(Ucluelet)

24

Cooper's Beach seems to be the unofficial name used by Ukee locals for the little pebbled cove that can be accessed from the Wild Pacific Trail. This stretch of coastline is famous for its dramatic storms and massive, pounding waves. Even when the wind is down and the rain is in remission, the ocean's energy rarely seems to abate. With dramatic black rock crags, and lichen-covered cedar forest clinging to the coastal bluffs, this section of the Pacific Rim has a deeply primordial feel to it. Hiking along the clifftop path, watching the heaving open ocean and crashing surf, you'd be forgiven for thinking it would be utter insanity to try to snorkel along here. However, Cooper's Beach offers a (relatively) tranquil pool that is largely shielded from the perpetual surge.

The beach itself is pebble-strewn, with the occasional pearly abalone shell adding a splash of West Coast colour. The swimming area is about 75 metres across, separated from the open ocean by a chain of offshore rocks that act as a natural granite breakwater. Underwater, the terrain is pebble in the shallows, with some sandy sections and moderate-sized boulders scattered throughout. The pool is only 5–6 metres at its deepest. The habitat here is rich—eelgrass beds, thick forests of giant kelp in the summertime, and carpets of pink feather coralline algae; all in all, a veritable smorgasbord for marine fauna. You will find a good selection of sea stars, anemones and nudibranchs here, as well as vast numbers of colourful top snails inhabiting the kelp fronds. The combination of its dramatic setting with the varied underwater flora and fauna makes this a West Coast winner.

Green surf anemone.

Signature species

Green surf anemones are by far the most common critter at Cooper's Beach. They are greatest in number along the left-hand edge of the pool, near the rocks that break the waves from the open ocean.

Critter list

Ochre star, leather star, blood star, sunflower star, bat star, rainbow star, drab six-armed star, giant California sea cucumber, orange cup coral, mauve lobed tunicate, mushroom compound tunicate, northern abalone, giant rock scallop, white berthella, noble sea lemon, yellow margin dorid, leopard dorid, kelp greenling, green surf anemone, brooding anemone, pink-tipped aggregating anemone, rose anemone, stubby rose anemone, black leather chiton, mossy chiton, red urchin, purple urchin.

Access

About a kilometre outside Ucluelet, the Ancient Cedars Trail connects the highway with the ocean. Consult www.wildpacifictrail.com for more information and a map of the full Wild Pacific Trail network. There is no formal parking lot here, but the verges on both sides of the highway have been widened and covered in gravel to allow cars to pull over.

There are two closely separated trailheads at the highway, which are designed to form a loop. A sign on the highway indicates one trail (the more southerly, closer to Ucluelet) as going to the Wild Pacific Trail, and identifies the more northerly path (which starts a few dozen metres farther along the highway) as the Ancient Cedars Trail. You can take either of these trails; the more southerly one is a bit more direct for accessing Cooper's Beach, but the more northerly one takes you past the eponymous old-growth trees.

Regardless of which trail you choose, an approximately five-minute (400-metre) walk takes you down a well-graded gravel path toward the ocean. When the path joins the main coast-hugging Wild Pacific Trail, take a left (south). Peering down through the trees on your right, you will see the pebble beach and its protected cove. Continue along the coast trail for another five minutes (300 metres) or so (if you hit the 6.5-kilometre marker, you have gone too far), whence a little-used path descends steeply through a cut in the rock. As you arrive on the beach, the snorkel area is on your right—it will be pretty obvious, as it will likely be the only bit of water that isn't in a frothing frenzy.

Tips

The depth here is only about 5–6 metres, depending on the tide, so don't worry too much about timing this with low water. Avoid the summertime, though, as the kelp growth is too thick to navigate freely.

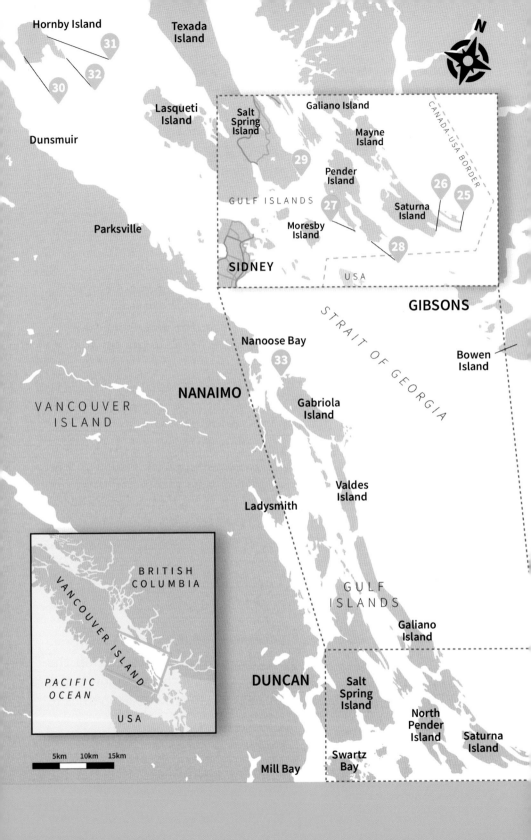

Hornby Island

31
32
30

Texada Island

N

Lasqueti Island

Salt Spring Island

Galiano Island

Mayne Island

Dunsmuir

CANADA-USA BORDER

29

Pender Island

26
25

GULF ISLANDS

27

Saturna Island

Parksville

Moresby Island

28

SIDNEY

USA

GIBSONS

STRAIT OF GEORGIA

Nanoose Bay

Bowen Island

33

NANAIMO

Gabriola Island

VANCOUVER ISLAND

Valdes Island

Ladysmith

BRITISH COLUMBIA

VANCOUVER ISLAND

GULF ISLANDS

Galiano Island

PACIFIC OCEAN

DUNCAN

Salt Spring Island

North Pender Island

USA

Saturna Island

Swartz Bay

5km   10km   15km

Mill Bay

THE GULF ISLANDS

25 EAST POINT / CLIFFSIDE (Saturna Island)

East Point is one of the gems in the crown of the Gulf Islands National Park Reserve, consisting of a dramatic rocky promontory with attractive sandstone and conglomerate cliffs that beg to be explored, both onshore and underwater. On the west side of the point, the land slopes gradually down to a protected bay with a picturesque sand/shell beach (Trillium Beach). The east side of the point is steeper but still walkable, with sandstone walls sculpted by the elements over the millennia. Between the two rocky shorelines is a pleasant grassy meadow, and the historic Fog Alarm Building (FAB) heritage centre. Seals and sea lions are a common sight in the shallows, with porpoises regularly cruising farther out.

The underwater topography from East Point toward the south starts with a pleasant mix of shallow shelves and flat sandy bottom, developing into vertiginous cliffs the farther along you go. In short, a wide variety of terrain and depths. This whole area experiences strong currents, which bring lots of food and hence the potential for plenty of good critters. However, in recent years the urchin population has gained a significant foothold (if urchins had actual feet) and has grazed much of the subsea rock surfaces bare. Still, these spiky critters are enjoyable in their own right (if you can suppress your concern for the kelp forests), and you'll find plenty of sea cucumbers and sea stars (mostly ochre, mottled and leather) to boot. For those comfortable with steep drops, head farther south to where the cliffs descend vertiginously (orcas cruise here within a stone's throw of the shore). For beginners, try the bay at Trillium Beach, where it's shallower and protected from current (but where there is consequently less wildlife to see).

Signature species

Orange sea pens—I can usually find one or two on the sandy flats below the FAB, but it requires a dive of at least 5 or 6 metres (more if the tide is high) to find them. Urchins are everywhere; the green variety in particular form huge carpets. Farther south (near the Cliffside entry point), the walls are covered with giant plumose anemones.

Critter list

Orange sea pen, giant California sea cucumber, orange sea cucumber, pale sea cucumber, black sea cucumber, armoured sea cucumber, leather star, ochre star, mottled star, striped sunstar, colourful six-armed star, drab six-armed star, blood star, red urchin, purple urchin, green urchin, yellow margin dorid, painted anemone, brooding anemone, pink-tipped aggregating anemone, giant plumose anemone, short plumose anemone, orange cup coral, giant Pacific chiton, black leather chiton, lined chiton, calcareous tube worm, kelp greenling, lingcod, copper rockfish, mauve lobed tunicate.

Orange sea pen.

Access

There is easy parking at the end of Tumbo Channel Road that serves the extended East Point area. Although there is room for some dozen or so cars, the parking can get busy in the summertime. There are two possible places to enter and exit the water. Option one is to take the trail to the right of the Parks Canada notice board (the trail to the left takes you down to Trillium Beach), toward the FAB, and enter from the rocks below. Follow the trail past the FAB to the point for the easiest way down. It's a few hundred metres' walk in total from the parking area. Option two is to take the 100-metre-long trail that cuts down to the water from the right-hand side of the parking area. This is a shorter walk, but there is a bit more of a scramble down to the water's edge. The FAB is not visible from here, and it's a few hundred metres' swim north to East Point.

Tips

Check the currents carefully—they can be fierce along this section, and back eddies don't always follow the main, predictable bulk tide flow. It is recommended to swim here shortly (an hour or so) before slack low tide, when the currents are usually calmest and the low waterline brings more critters into easy dive view. If the current is moving, you can consider making this a drift snorkel between the two entry points.

The steeper sections along East Point and Cliffside tend to stay relatively free of leafy vegetation, making this a good summer location. However, the shallower rocks at the northern tip tend to get covered with rockweed, so watch your step on the slippery surface. Did you know that you can squeeze the goo out of rockweed buds to make a natural sunscreen? I know, this guidebook is an oracle of useful information.

ECHO BAY
(Saturna Island)

26

Steep cliffs loom on both sides of this east-facing bay, which is part of the Gulf Islands National Park Reserve (adjacent to the camping area). Echo Bay is well protected from current and prevailing west winds; the waters here are almost always calm and this is a great spot for the beginner (as long as you don't mind the hike in). The bay itself has a sand-mud bottom and offers little of interest—snorkel along the rocky edges to enjoy the wildlife here. The two sides of the bay are quite different in their terrain and wildlife offerings. Heading out left from the beach takes you first over some shallow rocky reefs, where you can find anemones and several species of sea cucumber. Farther out, the cliff face becomes sheer and deep (deeper than I can see or dive), but is mostly barren for the snorkeller, with the exception of grazing urchins.

In my opinion, the right side of the bay offers much more of interest. The depth is perfect for snorkelling—mostly less than 5 metres or so, with lots of interesting boulders and undercuts where you can find carpets of zoanthids, tunicates and small sponges. Hundreds of sea cucumbers burrow into the rocky crevices and litter the bottom with orange, white and red. But the stars of the show are the huge colonies of giant plumose anemones at the far end of the bay, at a depth that is perfect for the snorkeller. Swimming here at a moderately low tide (less then 1.5 metres) will have these colonies at eye level, though still extending many metres below you for your diving pleasure.

Signature species

The last large boulder before the main cliff on the right-hand side from the beach has a particularly rewarding overhang, with a large colony of zoanthids, some big shiny sea squirts and colourful compound tunicates. But the main event at Echo Bay is the spectacular expanse of giant plumose anemones toward the point (follow the shore out to the right from the beach).

Critter list

Blood star, armpit blood star, sunflower star, leather star, vermilion star, drab six-armed star, ochre star, mottled star, rainbow star, giant California sea cucumber, armoured sea cucumber, pale sea cucumber, orange sea cucumber, giant plumose anemone, short plumose anemone, painted anemone, stubby rose anemone, giant white dorid, leopard dorid, Nanaimo dorid, yellow margin dorid, white-and-orange-tipped nudibranch, opalescent nudibranch, clown nudibranch, frosted nudibranch, white berthella, orange zoanthid, compound mushroom tunicate, shiny sea squirt, giant Pacific chiton, orange cup coral, green urchin, red urchin, purple urchin, lingcod, kelp greenling.

Access

Parking for Echo Bay is at the trailhead for access to the national park camping area at Narvaez Bay. From here, it is a 1-kilometre walk along a well-maintained trail down to the bay. It slopes gently downhill on the way to the beach, which of course translates to a bit of a trudge on the return journey. Echo Bay is on your right as you reach the base of the trail (which then curves around to the left toward the main campsite at Narvaez Bay).

Tips

Narvaez Bay is one of the few places on Saturna where you can camp, and the sites are reservable in advance through Parks Canada. It is a popular location in the summer months, though, so plan ahead if you intend to stay here (there is also overflow camping for walk-ins). There is considerable underwater vegetation here in the summertime (May–August) that covers the shallow rocks and sea floor, hiding much of the wildlife. However, the large colonies of giant plumose anemones on the right-hand cliffs keep their section of rock face clear, so are visible even at the height of the summer bloom. You can enjoy these giant plumose colonies even at fairly high tide, as long as the visibility is good. The highest tide I have snorkelled here is 3.5 metres, but I could still easily see all the giant plumose a couple of metres below me.

Orange zoanthids.

27 PETER COVE (Pender Island)

Located at the very tip of North Pender Island, the pincer-shaped Peter Cove is actually as far south as the southern coast of South Pender! The cove is sizable and consists of three subcoves separated by small, rocky points. All three can be traversed on foot at low tide. Swimming the full inner extent of Peter Cove's coastline is over half a kilometre, plus there is a little cluster of islets in the bay itself. All told, there is abundant real estate for the snorkeller to explore, and you will likely need several visits to do it justice.

The beach at Peter Cove is fine and pebbly, with the usual driftwood seating above the high tide line. Although it's unlikely to be busy, owing to its out-of-the-way location and limited parking, there are several houses whose gardens open right out onto the beach. As a result, Peter Cove feels less private than many Gulf Island beaches. From its high-tide pebble carpet, the shore descends into a shallow, sandy bay that is perfect for kiddies, as well as kayak launching. The rocky shoreline of the cove is fairly shallow, with no big drop-offs or intimidating topography. Indeed, if you come at low tide, you will have most of the interesting stuff more or less at eye level and barely need to do any diving at all. The islets in the middle of the bay are a favourite seal haul-out, and you are highly likely to observe marine mammals while in the water here.

Peter Cove is a worthy Gulf Island destination as a result of both its interesting and extensive topography, and its diverse small-scale invertebrate life. I once counted 10 species of nudibranchs in a single visit, including a rarely seen golden dirona. The sea

Golden dirona.

slug action can be found all around the rocky shallows, but I find the little point that separates the northernmost subcove from the other two to be particularly rewarding. There are also often nudibranchs to be found on the kelp, in the eelgrass and on the vegetation on the mooring buoys.

Critter list

Giant plumose anemone, short plumose anemone, painted anemone, Monterey dorid, Heath's dorid, noble sea lemon, clown nudibranch, Nanaimo dorid, yellow margin dorid, Hudson's dorid, opalescent nudibranch, golden dirona, shag-rug nudibranch, ochre star, leather star, drab six-armed star, mottled star, blood star, northern feather duster worm, polymorph feather duster worm, calcareous tube worm, black leather chiton, lined chiton, cross jelly, green urchin, giant acorn barnacle, shiny sea squirt, compound mushroom tunicate.

Access

At the very end of Plumper Way is a short, well-signposted access trail down to the beach at Peter Cove. There is very limited parking, just space enough for a couple of cars (be careful not to block any driveways). Moreover, the road is narrow, which limits verge-side parking opportunities; fortunately, this is not a spot that is thronged by the masses, so you are likely to be able to deposit your ride with minimal difficulty. There is clear signage for the public beach access; as on the rest of Pender, this is in the form of a metre-high wooden post. Descending the gently sloping steps for about 50 metres brings you to the southernmost of the three subcoves.

Tips

The cove is not terribly deep, and even with tide heights of 3 metres or so, divers of even modest ability will be able to enjoy much of the real estate. Check the sandy shallows for sole and flounder.

There are lots of mooring buoys in the cove, and the owners seem to be lackadaisical in their cleaning habits. As a result, you can often find mini-ecosystems growing on their undersides—search through the kelp leaves for nudibranchs.

The crescent shape of Peter Cove means that it is protected from the wind in most directions. There is also no current in the cove itself, making it ideal for beginners. But be aware that venturing around Wallace Point will put you into much faster water.

CRADDOCK BEACH
(Pender Island)

The south coast of South Pender Island is blessed with several lovely beaches with good public access. Coupled with the nutrient-rich currents that zip through Boundary Pass, and some wonderful underwater topography, this coastline is primed for a rewarding underwater experience. Craddock Beach, and specifically the small, rocky peninsula known as Tilly Point, is one of the most well-known Southern Gulf Island destinations for scuba divers. Luckily for us, the goodies that attract divers are also accessible to snorkellers as long as the tide is not too high.

When you arrive and look to your left, you'll see the pebble beach at Craddock extending in a graceful arc for a few hundred metres to the north, ending in sheer (but not very high) cliffs. Looking to your right, you'll notice a small pebble tombolo (submerged at high tide) that terminates in a small, unassuming rocky point. This is Tilly Point, which forms a C-shaped bay that offers pleasant snorkelling in protected waters. Here, you can find nudibranchs and smaller anemone species without having to worry about current exposure.

However, the main draw of Craddock Beach is on the outer, south-facing side of Tilly Point. Despite its unimpressive above-water extent, the small headland drops off quickly into the open ocean. A series of ledges and overhangs hosts a variety of wildlife that thrives in the current-swept pass. Most impressive of all is a series of caves (scuba divers are able to do a complete swim-through in one section) that are plastered with hundreds of giant plumose anemones. Even from the surface (at low tide), you will

Giant plumose anemones.

be able to peer into these cavernous tunnels, where the darkness of the crevasse contrasts with the ghostly white of the anemone inhabitants. Spooky.

Signature species
Hoards of giant plumose anemones.

Critter list
Short plumose anemone, giant plumose anemone, painted anemone, pink-tipped aggregating anemone, moonglow anemone, ochre star, leather star, colourful six-armed star, mottled star, blood star, armpit blood star, hooded nudibranch, Monterey dorid, frosted nudibranch, Nanaimo dorid, Hudson's dorid,

white-and-orange-tipped nudibranch, giant California sea cucumber, armoured sea cucumber, black leather chiton, cross jelly, moon jelly, comb jelly, red urchin, orange cup coral, giant rock scallop, shiny sea squirt.

Access

There is space for 10 or so cars in the widened dead end of Craddock Drive. Beach access is well signposted with one of the wooden trail markers that signal coastal access all around Pender. The trail is short, less than 100 metres, down steps cut into the ground (i.e., not too steep), emerging onto a pleasant pebble beach.

Once on the beach, you will see a small pebble tombolo that leads to a small, rocky outcrop (at high tides, the land bridge is submerged and you'll just see a small islet). The anemone-lined caverns are on the outer (southern) edge of this point.

Tips

The current can be very strong along this southern coast of Pender Island. I have also heard that there can be a significant downward undertow around the caves (although I haven't experienced any vertical currents personally), which is bad news for snorkellers and divers. The challenge is that the timing of slack tide (low current) here is rather unpredictable. Local advice is to arrive about an hour before the predicted Boundary Bay slack tide and judge the conditions as they evolve. Even if the current is moving at a moderate pace, you can still take advantage of the topography of Tilly Point; enter on the side of the pebble tombolo that allows you to drift with the current, and exit at the other side. This avoids the need to retrace your fin strokes and swim into the current.

The giant plumose anemones are definitely best viewed at relatively low tides; unless you are comfortable diving in the current, aim to visit when the water level is below 2 metres or so.

29 BEAVER POINT (Salt Spring Island)

One of the most popular destinations on Salt Spring is Ruckle Provincial Park, located a short drive from the Fulford Harbour ferry terminal. The 7 kilometres of shoreline and open grassy meadow make this a fantastic camping venue. There is also a working farm in the park (the Ruckle family donated land to BC Parks in 1972), which offers tours and accommodation. Snorkelling can be enjoyed pretty much anywhere along the park's coastline, but Beaver Point is established in the dive community, thanks to the fast-flowing, nutriment-carrying current to which it is exposed.

At Beaver Point, a series of small beaches notched into the sandstone shoreline offers a range of water entry options. Some of these beaches are perfect for swimming—shallow and sandy, though without much wildlife apart from gaper clams. These oversized bivalves are found throughout the sandy shallows, their dark, gaping throats looking ominous but also perfect for a mischievous poke.

Between the beaches are rocky headlands and short stretches of sculpted sandstone cliff. These rocky areas are where you'll find the interesting snorkelling terrain, with a range of depths and some fun underwater boulders and overhangs. Note that in the summer, this area is highly vegetated, and the beaches become a thick mass of seaweed and eelgrass.

Pink scallop. Notice the eyes around the mantle.

Critter list

Ochre star, leather star, mottled star, drab six-armed star, blood star, armpit blood star, short plumose anemone, pink-tipped aggregating anemone, painted anemone, orange sea cucumber, shiny sea squirt, orange cup coral, red urchin, gaper clam, pink scallop, giant rock scallop, giant Pacific chiton, black leather chiton, noble sea lemon, Monterey dorid, yellow margin dorid, Nanaimo dorid, clown nudibranch, frosted nudibranch, northern feather duster worm.

Access

Park in the well-signposted day-use area, located at the end of Beaver Point Road. There is space here for several tens of cars spread over a couple of lots. A metal gate bars further vehicle progress, but the paved path continues onward to connect with the ample trail network around the park.

There are several options for accessing beaches and exploring the coastline. Immediately on your left from the parking lot is a broad sand and pebble beach that is popular with families, thanks to its easy access and shallow bay. While it's a pleasant swimming beach, there is not much for snorkelling here. Instead, continue a few hundred metres along the paved trail to Beaver Point (a small information board has a short history of the location). On the left is a sand and shale beach, while on the right there is an alternative beach entry with a larger-pebble surface—choose your preferred terrain! From either access point, the more interesting underwater exploration is off to your right.

Tips

Ruckle Park is an excellent family destination and the campsite here is regularly full during the summer. There are also some fine swimming spots (such as the beach immediately by the day-use parking lot), a pleasant trail network and a farm.

There are a few potential marine hazards to be aware of. The currents at Beaver Point can get fairly strong, and the beaches can experience quite large waves from passing ferries. Boats seem to enjoy cutting close to shore here.

Salt Spring is a very popular destination, particularly for the Saturday market. As a result, Saturday morning ferries from Swartz Bay in the tourist season regularly fill up, so it's best to skip Saturdays for your snorkel day trips. Likewise, Sunday evenings are best avoided, as the crowds evacuate back to Victoria.

FORD'S COVE
(Hornby Island)

30

Just next to the marina, the sandstone shelves at Ford's Cove are one of Hornby Island's best-known snorkelling spots. Parking and water access are both easy, and this location is fairly sheltered from strong currents. The terrain is a blend of both sandstone shelves and sandy bottom, making this an interesting and varied spot with a good stock of wildlife. Away from the shoreline, several short drop-offs and undercuts are well populated by plumose anemones. Beyond the rocky foreshore, the mixed sand and pebble sea floor hosts a healthy eelgrass garden. After the herring spawn, the blades are caked with roe—an interesting annual event to witness, but be prepared for poor visibility for a few weeks afterward.

Signature species

Vermilion stars are very abundant here, and giant dendronotids are a fairly frequent sight.

Critter list

Ochre star, mottled star, leather star, vermilion star, drab six-armed star, clown nudibranch, giant dendronotid, Lewis's moon snail, Aleutian moon snail, short plumose anemone, moonglow anemone, pink-tipped aggregating anemone, painted anemone, giant California sea cucumber, orange sea cucumber, pale sea cucumber.

Vermilion star.

Access

There is plenty of parking just outside the marina, though it can be hard to find a spot in the summer (likewise, if you're planning to visit by boat, the dinghy tie-up space is very limited). To access the shoreline, take the few steps down to the sandstone shelves behind the marina office/store and head around the shoreline to your left (going right just takes you to the artificial seawall, which harbours less life). Enter anywhere that looks friendly given the tide height. There are some nice shelves and overhangs at the near end of this section, so it is good to venture away from the shore a little, but be very vigilant of boat traffic, which can be significant in the summer. Farther along is mostly sand and eelgrass (great for moon snails!).

Tips

Like the rest of the Gulf Islands, this location experiences quite extreme tide heights, in excess of 5 metres, a result of the massive volume of water that needs to be squeezed through the Strait of Georgia. If you are visiting from out of town, consult the tide tables to make sure you have some daytime low tides—5 extra metres of water are a lot to dive through.

Hornby Island is one of the most popular Gulf Island tourist destinations. As such, accommodation can be at a premium during the summer months, and the island can actually feel quite crowded (not to mention the ferry queues, which can reach epic lengths).

TRALEE POINT
(Hornby Island)

31

Lying on the north side of Hornby Island, Tralee Point is characterized by sandstone shelves and a small, sandy beach tucked in an east-facing nook in front of Sea Breeze Lodge. Wildlife isn't terribly varied here, but this is an excellent spot for enjoying moonglow anemones, which are abundant in both the bay and the numerous intertidal rock pools. This species is little seen on the more southerly Gulf Islands or around Victoria, so enjoying them here in such large numbers is a real treat. Although not a large species, or as showy in colour as rose or painted anemones, moonglows have a radiant quality that is utterly captivating—they may well become your new favourite cnidarian.

Signature species

Moonglow anemones are everywhere both in the sandy bay and on the rocky shelves. Indeed, at low tide, you can find them aplenty without even getting your feet wet, just by strolling around the tide pools.

Critter list

Ochre star, leather star, drab six-armed star, Monterey dorid, Nanaimo dorid, leopard dorid, short plumose anemone, moonglow anemone, pink-tipped aggregating anemone, orange sea cucumber, pale sea cucumber, lined chiton.

Access

The closest public access (and parking) is at the end of Fowler Road. Follow the short trail to the beach, and then walk left toward the point and continue around westward to find the sandy beach at the base of the cabins.

Tips

This spot is at its best when the tide is not too low, so that the sandstone shelves are still underwater and you can enjoy the anemones (unless, of course, you are hoping to enjoy them as a beachcomber). At low tide, there are still plenty to be seen in the sandy bay outside Sea Breeze Lodge.

Moonglow anemones.

In mid-March, the Hornby Island Conservancy (www.conservancyhornbyisland.org) organizes the annual HerringFest, a week-long celebration of all things herring. Enjoy the puns of the education classes at the "Herring School" and the nightlife of the "Herring Ball." The evenings are packed with musical entertainment, readings, art installations and ocean-based movie screenings.

FLORA ISLET

32

Flora Islet is located off the eastern tip of Hornby Island, separated from St. John's Point by only a few hundred metres. Part of Helliwell Provincial Park, Flora is characterized by sandstone conglomerate rock, with some scrubby vegetation on the higher ground, and a pleasant pebble beach at the north end. There is a substantial sea lion colony that favours the rocks at the southern end of the islet.

Flora is famous in the scuba diving community as one of the few locations where one can see sixgill sharks. Normally a deepwater species, these sharks used to frequent the (relative) shallows around Flora Islet in the summer months, at depths of only a few dozen metres. However, what used to be a reliable summer wildlife sight has apparently now become more of a rarity, even for scuba divers. Nonetheless, Flora remains a popular scuba location, with boat charters run by several local outfitters (e.g., in Nanaimo).

For the snorkeller, the main attraction at Flora is definitely the underwater topography. The south-facing side of the island descends in a series of shelves before dropping off to a steep wall that descends some 75 metres (hence the popularity as a dive site). Snorkellers, however, will be limited to the shelves, which nonetheless give ample exploration and depth opportunities. Numerous overhangs and ridges provide seemingly endless nooks and crannies to explore, even at shallow depths; it will suffice to merely invert yourself underwater to have access to such features and peer under protruding ledges.

Orange cup corals.

On the critter front, the diversity is modest—it will be mostly the red urchins, ochre stars and leather stars that dominate your check-list. There are small colonies of short plumose anemones, and I particularly enjoyed seeing the orange colour morphs, which are less common. Fish are fairly plentiful—numerous shoals of smaller species such as herring, and good numbers of rockfish hiding out under ledges.

Critter list

Mottled star, leather star, blood star, ochre star, vermilion star, copper rockfish, kelp greenling, blackeye goby, Pacific herring, yellow margin dorid, red urchin, giant California sea cucumber, orange sea cucumber, short plumose anemone, calcareous tube worm, orange cup coral, giant rock scallop, Lewis's moon snail.

Access

Although separated from St. John's Point on Hornby Island by only a few hundred metres, swim access to Flora is not recommended. First, it would require hiking for a couple of kilometres from the Helliwell parking lot, a distance considered by many lead-carrying snorkellers to be on the cusp between fun and tedium. Second, the water can move through that island gap at a fair clip, and it would be easy to get caught out as conditions change.

Instead, the recommended way to access Flora Islet is by boat. One option is to canoe or kayak here from Hornby; departure from

Tribune Bay would be the most obvious choice, a route that allows you to take in the sculpted sandstone artwork of the Helliwell cliffs. Alternatively, if you're approaching by motorized craft, it is a quick 13-kilometre dash from the Deep Bay boat launch on Vancouver Island, a route that takes you past the impressive Chrome Island Lighthouse, as well as snorkel-worthy blocks at Eagle Rock at the southern tip of Denman Island. However, beyond the extra sightseeing possibilities, the main benefit of a day trip from Vancouver Island by boat is avoiding the double-ferry jeopardy of getting to Hornby, which is a guaranteed way to waste hours of your time in the summer. Whether you arrive by kayak or motorized craft, the pebble beach at the north end of Flora is the natural place to land or anchor your boat in the shallows.

Tips

The south-facing shoreline of the islet tends to be much more protected than the north, where waves and chop can be noticeably more slappy on a given day. Indeed, this area can experience quite windy conditions, so check the forecast extra carefully before you set out.

There is very little vegetation along the Flora Islet coastline (probably owing to all of those red urchins!), which means that summertime snorkelling is relatively uncompromised. This is just as well, as the tide height difference in these waters is about 5 metres, so wintertime visits require navigating a significantly deeper water column.

If visiting Flora by boat from Deep Bay, carefully check the water levels at Point Atkinson when planning your trip. It turns out that Deep Bay is really not so deep, at least at the boat ramp, and you will need at least a 1-metre tide height to launch (and get out again!).

33 MALASPINA GALLERIES (Gabriola Island)

The Malaspina Galleries are a short section of dramatic, sculpted sandstone cliff at the western extent of Gabriola Island. A short access trail takes you through a grove of spruce and arbutus that opens out to a finger of rock pointing back toward Newcastle Island. Looking to the north, the dramatic coastal mountains loom above the Sunshine Coast, frosted in snow for much of the year. From the point, as you look back in the direction you came from, you will see the famous sandstone "wave" that has been carved into the friable shoreline. All in all, this is a delightful spot, and the short (20-minute) ferry ride from downtown Nanaimo, and the even shorter (five-minute) drive from the Gabriola terminal, make this an easy half-day trip from Vancouver Island's second largest city.

The sandstone cliffs extend only 5–7 metres underwater. On the walls themselves, you will find plentiful ochre, leather and mottled stars, as well as clusters of short plumose anemones, though the overall species diversity is rather limited. Nonetheless, the dramatic geology and protected waters make this a pleasant spot that is good for beginners.

Critter list

Ochre star, leather star, mottled star, drab six-armed star, short plumose anemone, pink-tipped aggregating anemone, leopard dorid, Monterey dorid, frosted nudibranch, orange sea cucumber.

Pink-tipped aggregating anemones.

Access

Parking for the Malaspina Galleries is (predictably) at the western extent of Malaspina Drive. There is no actual parking lot here, just a slightly widened section of the road as it does a sharp U-turn loop. There is signage aplenty to indicate the verboten parking areas, limiting the visitor to some half a dozen opportunities between private driveways. Park nose first (not parallel) to maximize the space.

The approach to the water is via a 100-metre-long trail between waterfront properties, through a narrow wooded section. Taylor Bay is on your right, but follow the trail straight ahead to get to the Galleries. Fences and warnings discourage clambering down the fragile overhanging sandstone cliffs. Instead, continue out to the point, which has a gentle descent to the water.

Tips

Snorkelling here can create considerable interest from the local sea lion population, especially during the winter months. Be cautious as these mammals are immense and (in contrast to harbour seals) bold and assertive with snorkellers.

Other worthwhile Gabriola destinations include Berry (Orlebar) Point and Logan Bay in Drumbeg Provincial Park.

N

POWELL
RIVER

COURTNEY

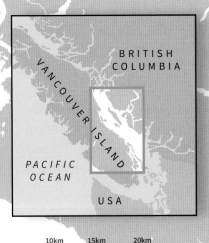

Texada
Island

Denman
Island   Hornby
Island

Lasqueti
Island

PORT
ALBERNI

PARKSVILLE

NANAIMO

SECHELT

STRAIT OF GEORGIA

Gabriola
Island

LADYSMITH

Galiano
Island

Cowichan Lake

DUNCAN

VANCOUVER ISLAND

Salt
Spring
Island

10km   15km   20km

COWICHAN TO COMOX

34 MAPLE BAY

The small town of Maple Bay is located in the beautiful Cowichan Valley about halfway between Victoria and Nanaimo. The Sansum Narrows separate Vancouver Island from Salt Spring Island, which looms large a couple of kilometres across the bay. Although currents can be strong through the narrows, Maple Bay itself offers a protected natural harbour, and is consequently popular with boaters and kayakers. The long pebble beach (technically, Maple Bay Beach Park) is almost half a kilometre long and a popular swimming spot in the summer. One could wade in from any part of the beach for a little snorkel session, though the monotonous pebble terrain is not terribly interesting. Still, you'll likely find a few scattered sea stars and maybe even a giant dendronotid, which seem to like the shallows of Maple Bay.

The more appealing option, as long as there is no boat traffic, is to cruise around the pilings of the municipal wharf. The depth of these pilings ranges from just a few metres close to shore to about 7 metres at the end of the wharf (depending on the tide, of course, which varies by 4 metres or so in the Sansum Narrows). On these vertical posts you'll find abundant plumose anemones and clusters of ochre stars, as well as all manner of macro life such as compound tunicates and delicate pink-tipped anemones along the edges of the wharf. If you like the idea of wreck diving, there are several submerged boats around the wharf in only 5 metres or so of water, though there is not much life growing on them yet.

Again, with the caveat of boat traffic, you can continue about 10 metres due east from the end of the wharf to find the "bottle field." Presumably, this is the accumulated detritus of drunken bottle-tossing contests from the end of the wharf. Despite the unnatural state of this seascape, it is quite fun to see the hundreds of barnacled bottles scattered on the sea floor, and wildlife will often make their homes therein. This section is deeper, though, and requires dives of at least 10 metres, even when the tide is low.

Signature species

Giant dendronotids are a relatively frequent find here, cruising along the pebbly bottom as they browse the tube-dwelling anemone buffet.

Lewis's moon snails (top) and their egg coils (bottom) are a frequent find in sandy shallows.

Critter list

Ochre star, mottled star, leather star, giant pink star, giant dendronotid, northern feather duster worm, calcareous tube worm, lined compound tunicate, pink-tipped aggregating anemone, short plumose anemone, tube-dwelling anemone, Lewis's moon snail, Pacific sea peach.

Access

From the municipal wharf parking lot, descend a short set of half a dozen steps just to the right of the dock. The steps deposit you directly onto the finely pebbled beach, whence you can simply tiptoe into the water.

Tips

Given the proximity to an active wharf, swimmers at Maple Bay should be extremely cautious about boat traffic. There is some awareness of thalassophiles among the locals; not only is the beach a popular swimming destination in the summer, but Maple Bay is also a popular scuba diving spot. Nonetheless, it is not recommended to snorkel near the dock in the summertime. I like to come here in the dead of winter, when the wharf is little used. However, even when the boat traffic is quiet, take extra precautions to be visible—take turns with your snorkel buddies to dive and keep watch, and consider using a float or buoy for extra visibility.

NECK POINT PARK
(Nanaimo)

Jutting out into the Strait of Georgia, Neck Point is a popular urban park in Nanaimo. The park takes its name from the double beach tombolo that extends like a neck from its north end, spreading out into a series of rocky outcrops that form a T shape above the beach. Extending over some 36 acres, Neck Point is an appealing mix of pebble beaches, volcanic rocks and Garry oak groves. Trails criss-cross the peninsula (a circumambulation of which is approximately 2 kilometres), and interpretative signs provide info on the flora and fauna of the park and its shoreline. All in all, a great family destination, whether for a picnic, a forest stroll or some beachcombing.

Neck Point is also well known as a premier Nanaimo scuba dive location. Although snorkellers will not be descending to equivalent depths, the approach and general area of exploration are the same, namely the islets at the top end of the "neck." Although the depth immediately below these islets is only 5–10 metres, you will not have to venture far from the shore to be hitting 20 metres, hence the popularity with the scuba set. With numerous mini-islands, as well as underwater walls and ridges, the terrain is perfect for snorkellers who are comfortable with a bit of diving.

In terms of critter sightings, ochre, leather and mottled stars dominate the invertebrate playbook, and there are good numbers of fish in the shallows. Those able to dive a bit deeper will discover walls of giant plumose anemones—mostly white, but with the occasional bright orange colour morph. The gravel bottom is the

The blood star (left) and armpit blood star (right) differ only in the conspicuous absence or presence of pale colouration around the central disk.

ideal habitat for tube-dwelling anemones, and you might be lucky enough to spot an orange sea pen, though this requires a dive of at least 7 metres.

Critter list

Short plumose anemone, tube-dwelling anemone, pink-tipped aggregating anemone, armpit blood star, ochre star, giant pink star, leather star, mottled star, copper rockfish, kelp greenling, painted greenling, lingcod, bay pipefish, blackeye goby, noble sea lemon, modest cadlina, yellow margin dorid, red urchin, orange sea pen, giant California sea cucumber, orange sea cucumber, moon jelly, northern abalone.

Access

There is parking for several dozen cars at the main lot. However, this is a popular location, and on summer days the parking area is buzzing. Having secured your spot, you can choose your snorkel access point anywhere along the peninsula, including from the beach immediately adjacent to the parking lot or from any of several points along the trail. However, I recommend making the short (400-metre or so) walk toward the eponymous "neck" and entering the water from one of the twin beaches there. The trail is somewhat undulating and there are stairs; as you are strolling with your minimal gear, feel sorry for the scuba divers who have to lug dozens of kilos of tanks and weights out here. You'll know that you are almost at the beach access when you scale a rather substantial staired boardwalk that looks down over the tombolo.

Tips

Departing from one of the neck's beaches, you can do a tour of all the rocky outcrops in a loop without having to retrace your steps (or fin strokes). The beach's neck is so narrow that you can depart from one side and return to the other, and then walk mere steps to recover your footwear. The snorkel loop is about 400 metres, beach to beach.

I find the outer section of the T, toward the northwest, to be the most rewarding, particularly if you have some dive capability. There are several sizable colonies of plumose anemones here, and in the sandy gravel bed (7–10 metres or so down, depending on the tide) you will find tube-dwelling anemones and the occasional orange sea pen.

36 JESSE ISLAND

Jesse Island is a 3.5-hectare private island in Departure Bay, just off the coast of suburban Nanaimo. Oriented primarily along an east-west axis, the south side of the island descends gently from a tree-crested summit through a grassy slope and finishes in a rocky foreshore. But it is the 400-metre-long north side of the island that is of appeal to the snorkeller. As you stare across from your Vancouver Island start point, you will already be able to see why the terrain on the north shore of Jesse Island is ideal—steep sandstone walls drop vertically down to the ocean. Indeed, once you have made the 200-metre swim across the channel, these cliffs instantly deliver—you will be greeted at Jesse by a wall full of short plumose anemones that coat the rock all the way to the bottom, about 5 metres below.

But these cliffs are just the beginning: Jesse Island boasts some of the most interesting snorkel terrain I have encountered anywhere around Vancouver Island. There are ledges, overhangs, big submerged boulders and—my favourite—a narrow canyon to swim through. As a result of both the wildlife and geology, Jesse Island is one of my favourite snorkel locations in the Nanaimo area.

Signature species

Walls covered with short plumose anemones! Although I wouldn't say that Jesse Island is particularly good for nudibranchs, I saw more here than at other locations in this chapter, including quite a few really big Monterey dorids.

Critter list

Ochre star, leather star, mottled star, armpit blood star, giant pink star, Monterey dorid, noble sea lemon, modest cadlina, short plumose anemone, tube-dwelling anemone, fried egg jelly, moon jelly, blackeye goby, painted greenling, kelp greenling, pile perch, Pacific herring, lined compound tunicate, gaper clam, calcareous tube worm.

Access

The place to park is along Stephenson Point Road. A very small pullout (with room for two cars) is on your right (if you're approaching from Hammond Bay Road), next to a fairly well-hidden Beach Access sign. The closest house number (on the opposite side of the street) is 3331. If both parking spaces are taken, there are a few places along the road you can pull into.

From the pullout, there is a steep set of stairs that descends to the shoreline (the hike back up will serve as a quick and free test of whether you have an undiagnosed heart condition). Once at the bottom, a very short descent on some boulders takes you to the pebble shoreline. It is a 200-metre swim to the other side. If you don't fancy the crossing under your own fin-power, dive shops in Nanaimo can arrange to bring snorkel groups here on a boat tour.

Jesse Island is private— you must not use the boat dock at the west end or land on the

Sea stars have the ability to regenerate lost limbs. This giant pink star (which is normally five-armed) seems to be growing extra appendages just for the fun of it.

island. A sign midway along the north shore cheerfully broad-casts that guard dogs are on duty.

Tips

My favourite part of a visit to Jesse is at the west end (where the boat dock is located), which will likely be your arrival point after your swim crossing. As you swim east along the coast after viewing the anemone-covered wall, you will soon encounter a small canyon that you can swim through on all but the lowest tides. The walls loom some 10 metres above you, but the canyon is only a few metres wide. There are lots of sea stars in here, and I also found several Monterey dorids and noble sea lemons, including some big egg coils laid on the rock wall.

The channel between Vancouver Island and Jesse Island does not seem much used by boat traffic, though I did see several Jet Skis (arguably, even more dangerous) charge past while I was visiting. Make sure you transit with care and vigilance. For the return crossing, you can use the large white Cable sign on the Vancouver Island side as a point to aim for.

Jesse Island ends up requiring a fair bit of swimming—200 metres across the channel, 400 metres from the west to east end, and then all the same again in reverse. The overall distance means that this is probably not a great option for beginners, who may not have calibrated their abilities.

SEA CUCUMBERS

In contrast to the large and obvious giant California sea cucumber, many sea cucumber species prefer to hide in rock crevices, showing only their feeding tentacles. The photos here show three common species (orange, armoured and stiff-footed), as seen either from above (tentacle view) or side-on (body view).

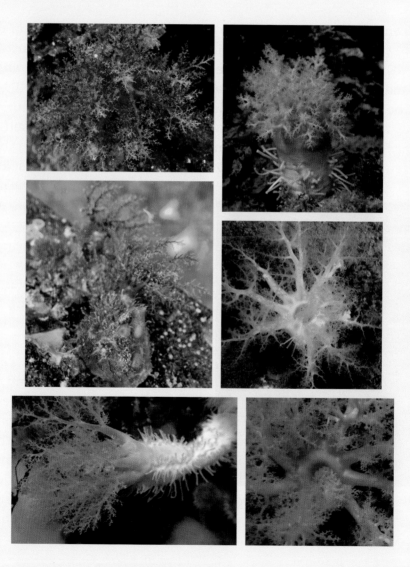

37 BLUEBACK COMMUNITY PARK (Nanoose Bay)

Sometimes also referred to as "Tyee" (due to its location off Tyee Crescent), Blueback is a compact community park in a residential part of Nanoose Bay. This is a popular spot with Nanaimo-based scuba divers, and these bubble blowers are likely to be the majority of the people you encounter at this diminutive but well-provisioned suburban beach access. The park itself is only about 50 metres wide, and consists of a single picnic table, a few trees for shade, and a nice cedar shelter that offers a space for changing and a portable toilet. The beach area is similarly dinky, only a few tens of metres wide, with the standard collection of driftwood at the high tide line. Overall, unless you are planning to take a dip, there is not much to keep you busy on land.

The underwater real estate, on the other hand, is quite extensive. The rocky reefs, boulders and short walls in the top 10 metres make this a varied and interesting landscape for snorkel exploration. Indeed, it is the varied submarine topography that is one

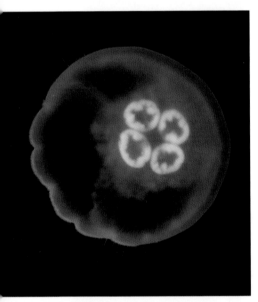

The four distinctive crescent shapes of the moon jelly are its gonads.

Giant California sea cucumber.

of the most attractive features of this location. The other notable aspect of snorkelling at Blueback is the high abundance of fish, often in sizable schools near the surface. In good conditions, it feels almost tropical! And don't forget to poke around in the rock crevices in search of greenling and rockfish. Invertebrate life is somewhat more limited—lots of the common sea star species but not much diversity.

Critter list

Short plumose anemone, calcareous tube worm, pale sea cucumber, giant California sea cucumber, orange sea cucumber, blackeye goby, pile perch, shiner perch, kelp greenling, copper rockfish, Pacific herring, ochre star, mottled star, leather star, vermilion star, blood star, armpit blood star, Monterey dorid, noble sea lemon, yellow margin dorid, white berthella, shiny sea squirt, lined compound tunicate, giant rock scallop, red urchin.

Access

There are six parking spots directly adjacent to the park, with space for several more vehicles on the grass verges opposite. Unless there is a dive class meeting here (it's a popular spot for beginners), you are unlikely to have trouble snagging a spot. From the parking area, it is a short (few dozen metres') walk down the side of the grassy park to the beach.

Tips

The marching armies of scuba divers who frequent this spot have cleared a boulder/barnacle-free path down the right-hand side of the beach. Although you will still be walking over pebbles, the booty-shredding variety has been largely moved aside.

In my opinion, the most interesting terrain is found by heading directly out (perpendicular) from the beach. A natural chute cuts through the rock—follow this to the right for some fun reefs of varied depth. In general, I find the right-hand side of the bay of more interest than the left.

OAK LEAF
(Nanoose Bay)

The original Oak Leaf Drive was a short spur leading off Dolphin Drive until some savvy developer spied this as the latest money-making opportunity in Nanoose Bay. The road has now been extended several hundred metres toward the north, with ritzy new houses being lined up along the waterfront. But this development has been good news for scuba divers, as the new approach (*avec* parking lot) puts them within tank-lugging distance of the beach. The rocky headland at the point and the beach that extends for several hundred metres to the north are now designated as a community park.

The obvious snorkel route takes you from the main beach around the point to the right. The gradient drops quite steeply; from the north tip of the point, the depth bottoms out at around 7–10 metres, depending on the tide. Search these sandy depths for tube-dwelling anemones, and maybe you'll get lucky and find a giant dendronotid on the prowl. Continuing around the point, you'll see several more walls that drop away, making this an excellent location for those who want to dive a little deeper. A scattering of giant plumose anemones can be found down here; although they're not in the dense colonies found at some locations, their height and deep orange colour are worth the dive. Alternatively, if you prefer the shallows, search for nudibranchs on tunicates, sponges and vegetation. I particularly enjoyed the peach-coloured frosted nudibranchs as a contrast to the usual white variety. Fish are less abundant here than at other nearby locations (such as Blueback and Neck Point parks).

The frosted nudibranch (white-lined dirona) is usually white but can appear in a variety of pastel shades.

Critter list

Mottled star, ochre star, leather star, blood star, vermilion star, giant pink star, frosted nudibranch, yellow margin dorid, giant dendronotid, hooded nudibranch, tube-dwelling anemone, short plumose anemone, giant plumose anemone, red urchin, green urchin, shiny sea squirt, lined compound tunicate, giant California sea cucumber, orange sea cucumber, giant rock scallop, northern abalone, moon snail, kelp greenling, painted greenling, blackeye goby, Pacific herring, shiner perch, pile perch, calcareous tube worm, lined chiton.

Access

The newly extended Oak Leaf Drive ends in a turning circle, with a gravel parking lot tucked down a ramp access into the forest. There is space for 10 cars or so. The only other patrons you are likely to encounter here are the scuba set (new homeowners in the development are too busy sitting at their granite countertops, sipping espresso and feeling smug). A lovely forest trail leads about 100 metres out to the point. Several side trails lead off to various water access points. If you bear to the right, you will come to a small, east-facing beach that offers an easy entry option. Alternatively, stick to the main trail until it leans to the left and deposits you on the main beach to the west of the point. This main beach offers the advantage that, being tucked behind the point, it is largely sheltered from any current.

Tips

The current can pick up along this section of the coastline, which is a bit more exposed to wind and waves than some other Nanoose locations, so assess conditions appropriately.

39 COTTAM POINT (Nanoose Bay)

Looking out to the impressively steep-sided Mistaken Island, Cottam Point is one of the most popular Nanoose Bay scuba dive spots. However, for snorkelling, the wildlife is not as abundant here as it is at other nearby locations. There seems to be markedly fewer fish than at Beachcomber Regional Park, despite the fact that the two locations are immediate neighbours. The most abundant critters I see at Cottam Point are urchins—large carpets of the green variety seem to be gaining a worrying monopoly over large tracts of the intertidal zone. Betty Pratt-Johnson's famous guidebook on scuba diving in the Pacific Northwest, *151 Dives*, describes the rich bull kelp growth here, but I saw nary a frond and was left wondering whether these spiky gluttons have been responsible for the apparent deforestation. Nonetheless, you can find all the usual suspects here, including the common sea star varieties and other small invertebrates, and this location can be easily combined with a visit to Beachcomber Regional Park (next entry).

Critter list

Ochre star, leather star, mottled star, armpit blood star, vermilion star, short plumose anemone, tube-dwelling anemone, painted anemone, pink-tipped aggregating anemone, kelp greenling, painted greenling, Pacific herring, blackeye goby, giant California sea cucumber, orange sea cucumber, red urchin, green urchin, calcareous tube worm, northern abalone, giant rock scallop, orange cup coral, lined compound tunicate.

Once abundant in BC's intertidal zone, ochre stars were a major casualty of the sea star wasting disease that hit in 2013. Fortunately, they are making a strong comeback and can once again be found splattered around the shallows in shades of pink, purple and orange. If you see one doing a handstand, it is not a spot of sea star yoga, but a spawning pose.

Access

Just as Marina Way runs out of land and has to turn back on itself, Seadog Road makes a final break for freedom to the tip of Cottam Point. There is space for a few cars to park at the end of the street, or along the verges, but it doesn't take more than half a dozen cars for this little cul-de-sac to feel crowded.

At the end of the street, a few rock steps lead out to the gently sloping shore—a nice short walk that makes this a popular location with scuba divers. However, the water entry can be a little tricky. There's quite a bit of slippery green stuff, so watch your step and try to find a smooth rock patch to lower yourself in.

Tips

If the wind is whipping up the surf here, try retreating around the coast to Beachcomber Regional Park, which tends to be more sheltered (and is a better overall destination to boot, in my humble snorkelling opinion). The current can also be moderately strong here.

TUNICATES

Tunicates, commonly referred to as sea squirts, are a diverse and colourful crew. Defined by their dual siphon structure, tunicates are filter feeders that can be solitary, social or compound. The in-and-out siphons of larger solitary species (such as the shiny sea squirt) are obvious; in compound species, they are mere pinprick openings in the sprawling colony.

40 BEACHCOMBER REGIONAL PARK (Nanoose Bay)

Just south of Cottam Point is Beachcomber Regional Park. Although you could combine these two locations in one long swim, they have their own entry points and distinct characters, so I have described them separately in this guide. Beachcomber Park itself is a small, forested area with a handful of short trails through the arbutus down to your choice of two pleasant pebble beaches: one north- and one south-facing. Between these two is a rocky shelf that slopes off gently to the water and is a popular fishing spot. What you can't tell from the land (and why it is popular with the fisherfolk) is that once below the surface, the terrain drops down sharply to depths of 8–10 metres just beyond the shoreline. This whole section is a fairly steep wall with plentiful cracks and overhangs, making it some of the most interesting terrain on the Nanoose peninsula.

There are excellent numbers of fish here—lots of greenling and rockfish, as well as smaller species such as herring and goby. On the walls themselves you'll find giant rock scallops, beautiful abalone and the snaking white cases of calcareous tube worms topped with fans of crimson and cream. Not too many nudibranchs here (mostly just a handful of yellow margins), though I did spot a giant dendronotid sitting down on the sandy bottom at about 9 metres' depth.

Painted greenling.

Signature species

There are lots of fish at Beachcomber. The prettily coloured kelp greenling is upstaged only by its show-off sibling, the painted greenling. Make sure you check under overhangs and crevices on the wall, as many species like to hang out in these rocky hideaways and will often allow you to get fairly close (which, of course, has not been good for their numbers in the face of the growing sport of spearfishing).

Critter list

Ochre star, leather star, mottled star, blood star, short plumose anemone, tube-dwelling anemone, kelp greenling, painted greenling, blackeye goby, copper rockfish, Pacific herring, orange sea cucumber, giant California sea cucumber, yellow margin dorid, giant dendronotid, northern abalone, giant rock scallop, red urchin, green urchin, calcareous tube worm, shiny sea squirt.

Access

Just before Marina Way does its about-turn at Cottam Point, signs on the left of the road announce that you are at Beachcomber Regional Park (although these will be obscured if the parking area is full). There is space for about a dozen cars to park along the roadside; this is a popular place on the weekend, and if you are here on a sunny summer afternoon, you may have to look farther along Marina Way for space. An indication of its popularity: signs are posted warning you not to leave valuables in your car.

There are a few trail options from the parking area, some steeper than others, but they all ultimately take you down to the foreshore in a hundred metres or so (scuba divers tend to find this all a bit much, bless them, and prefer Cottam Point, where the walk is much shorter). You can enter the water from either of the pebble beaches, but that adds unnecessarily to the swim. Since the rock shelf is easy to navigate on foot (flat, smooth and fairly vegetation-free), it is just as easy to walk to the water's edge here and drop right in where the wall descends.

Tips

Watch out for fisherfolk on the shore and respect one another's right to share the coastline. When I visited, there didn't seem to be too much underwater risk of old lures and line, but always be vigilant when you know that there is active recreational line fishing.

MADRONA POINT
(Nanoose Bay)

Madrona Point is octopus central for scuba divers. Unfortunately, giant Pacific octopus dens are usually significantly deeper than most snorkellers can dive. But even without the likelihood of a cephalopod encounter, Madrona Point is a decent spot in Nanoose Bay for those who stick to modest depths.

Emerging from the forest path, the conglomerate rock shoreline at Madrona Point sweeps out a wide shelf to both the left and right. The most satisfying snorkel terrain is off to the left, where you will find the so-called "small wall." This wall drops down fairly vertically (even slightly over-hanging in parts) to about 5–8 metres, and is richly cov-ered with short plumose anemones, ochre stars and leather stars. It is not a long section, and by the time you round the corner of the point the terrain becomes more gradual, sloping off to a sandy bottom that starts at about 5 metres depth. This is the

Tube-dwelling anemone.

ideal habitat for tube-dwelling anemones, which are extremely abundant here. As you move around to the northern side of the point, there are some boulders and small reefs where you'll find more sea stars.

For those who want to try their hand at the "main wall," where the wolf-eels, octopuses and scuba divers hang out, head north from the point—look for the round white dive buoy that marks the top of the wall drop. But exploring the main wall requires dives of 15–20 metres or more.

Signature species

Tube-dwelling and stubby rose anemones abound on the sandy bottom straight out from the tip of Madrona Point, at depths as shallow as 4 metres (depending on the tide).

Critter list

Ochre star, leather star, mottled star, giant pink star, short plumose anemone, tube-dwelling anemone, pink-tipped aggregating anemone, stubby rose anemone, kelp greenling, bay pipefish, copper rockfish, blackeye goby, lined chiton, giant California sea cucumber, yellow margin dorid.

Access

Park at the far end of Madrona Drive—there is room for a couple of cars right at the trailhead, as well as space enough for four cars in a small gravel area on the right, and ample space along the residential street's verges. It can get quite busy here with the scuba crowd on the weekends, so make sure you always park respecting the private property of this residential area.

The trailhead may be hidden by parked cars, but it is right at the end of the street, next to the sign that prohibits campfires (make sure you are not waltzing down a private driveway!). The path is flat but narrow, cutting through the woods between two waterfront homes. After just a few tens of metres, you will pop right out at the beach.

Once you hit the beach, take a hard left and go as far as you can along the shore in this direction. When you can't go left anymore, where the waterfront gardens meet the water at the southwestern extent of the point, you will see a deep cut in the rock. Use this channel to enter the water and then turn right. This deposits you almost immediately on the small wall.

Tips

Although the octopus dens here are mostly along the main wall, you might get lucky at shallower depths. Divers I met when I visited here told me they had just seen one in only 3 metres of water. If you spot a preponderance of discarded crab shells along any of the rock walls at Madrona Point, you may be close to an octo hideout.

The small wall isn't very deep, so if you have good wintertime visibility, the daytime high tides shouldn't limit your enjoyment here too much. However, this location can be quite exposed if the wind is blowing from the north, and wave action is likely to be the biggest limiting factor in the winter.

42 ROYSTON SHIPWRECKS

Many a ship has come to a grisly end along the coast of Vancouver Island. However, the nautical graveyard at Royston is man-made and dates back to the 1930s, when ships were deliberately sunk here to provide protection for log booms against the wind and waves. The fleet was gradually added to over the course of a few decades, and there are now over a dozen ships spread over several hundred metres on the eastern side of a boulder breakwater. Many of these are sizable vessels, including three frigates and a pair of naval destroyers, as well as several barques, tugs and even old harpoon boats. Although much of the ships' shells have rusted away over the decades, huge chunks of metallic carcass can still be seen above the waterline. For the snorkeller, the underwater view is even more dramatic, as thousands of plumose anemones have anchored themselves on the rusty remains, like tiny

Short plumose anemones and ochre stars, ahoy!

spectres haunting these ghost ships. Although the wildlife here is very limited in its diversity, snorkelling around these shallow wrecks is a memorable experience.

Signature species

Short plumose anemones coat every rusty hull and piling. Platoons of moon snails cruise around the sandy shallows.

Critter list

Short plumose anemone, moonglow anemone, lined chiton, mossy chiton, orange sea cucumber, crystal jelly, ochre star, mottled star, Lewis's moon snail.

Access

The approach to the wrecks is at the end of Hilton Road, off Highway 19A. From the spacious gravel parking lot, follow the trail some 200 metres to the end of the breakwater (or choose a spot anywhere along it, depending on what looks tide-friendly).

Tips

The area around the wrecks is shallow and their carcasses reach above even the highest tide line, so waiting for a low tide is not necessary. Indeed, low tides bring the challenge of sharp edges just below the surface. You should avoid touching any of these wrecks, not only to protect this historical site, but also to avoid the potential of a nasty cut (even if your tetanus shots are up to date!). I recommend coming here when the tide is no lower than about 3 metres.

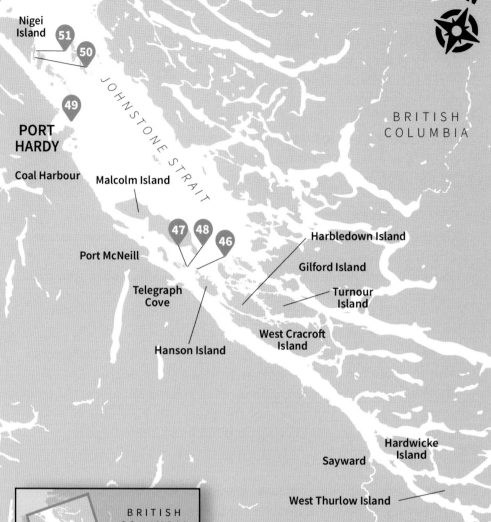

N

Nigei
Island
51
50

49

PORT
HARDY

Coal Harbour

Malcolm Island

47 48 46

Port McNeill

Telegraph
Cove

Hanson Island

JOHNSTONE STRAIT

BRITISH
COLUMBIA

Harbledown Island

Gilford Island

Turnour
Island

West Cracroft
Island

Hardwicke
Island

Sayward

West Thurlow Island

East Thurlow Island

VANCOUVER
ISLAND

Sonora Island

Quadra
Island

44
45
Campbell
Lake
43
CAMPBELL
RIVER

BRITISH
COLUMBIA

VANCOUVER ISLAND

PACIFIC
OCEAN

USA

5km   10km   15km

THE NORTH ISLAND (Campbell River and Beyond)

43 ARGONAUT WHARF (Campbell River)

Argonaut Wharf is *the* classic Campbell River shore dive for scuba folks and it's pretty bloomin' amazing for snorkellers as well. There are many reasons why Argonaut Wharf should be high on your snorkel hit list. First, it is one of the few locations in the North Island that does not require a boat; indeed, I would rate it as one of the best shore snorkels on Vancouver Island. Second, it is vegetation-free in the summer, when the South Island is covered with leafy greens. Finally, the need to snorkel here following a high tide (to avoid the vicious back eddies that rip through Discovery Passage) makes Argonaut Wharf conducive to wintertime visits, when the visibility can be fabulous.

The wharf itself is an industrial structure located behind the strip malls of Campbell River. The above-water monstrosity gives way to incredible underwater beauty, where the life-covered pilings descend 10–15 metres to a sandy bottom. Swimming around these underwater structures is like exploring a waterlogged forest; staring down the anemone-laden trunks feels like an inverted vista up toward the forest canopy. So, while the species list below might seem a bit thin, the sheer abundance of anemones and colour at Argonaut Wharf makes snorkelling here a truly memorable experience.

Although your eye will be drawn by the massive colonies of giant plumose anemones, there are also plentiful populations of short plumose and painted anemones. If you're able to dive a little deeper, you may also find the occasional crimson beauty. You'll also be treated to some sizable ochre stars, and if you're lucky you might catch sight of a giant dendronotid. Although these are most commonly seen on the sea floor, searching for a tube-dwelling anemone snack, you may also find them swimming near the surface.

Signature species

Plumose (giant and short) and painted anemones.

Critter list

Giant plumose anemone, short plumose anemone, painted anemone, crimson anemone, ochre star, mottled star, blood star, armpit blood star, giant dendronotid, northern feather duster worm, northern staghorn bryozoan, orange cup coral, green urchin, lion's mane jelly.

Giant dendronotid in two different colour varieties.

Access

The approach to Argonaut Wharf is along Spit Road, just a short distance off Highway 19A, and avoids any need to navigate downtown Campbell River. There is a small dirt parking lot on the beach side of the road, opposite the RV park, with space enough for a half dozen cars. The beach is long and pebbly, and the swim out to the first pilings is about 100 metres. The central section hosts more wildlife than the outer pilings.

Tips

The key to snorkelling at Argonaut Wharf is timing with the currents. Discovery Passage experiences strong back eddies that mean that slack water does not (necessarily) correspond with low/high tide. In fact, the local intel is that the best time to snorkel the wharf is from about two hours after high tide (according to the Campbell River tide chart) up until about two hours before low tide. Note that on some days this gives a window of several hours, but on other days the tide turns more quickly. So you'll need to always check the time of both the high tide before, as well as the low tide following, the time you plan to dive. Now, I know what you're thinking, that snorkellers usually preach the gospel of low tide excursions in order to enjoy the best wildlife views in the lower tidal zones. However, even at fairly high tide (I was there when the Campbell River table was showing almost 3 metres), as long as the visibility is decent, you will be able to enjoy the underwater show.

If you are diving, keep your eyes on the surface as you ascend, as some of the wharf's crossbeams jut out at angles just below the waterline, and bumping your head upon surfacing is both unpleasant and potentially dangerous. I like to ascend with my arm extended above my head so I can feel for any obstacles as I come up.

MAY ISLAND

A mere 200 metres in length, May Island is a modest crop of rock nestled up against the western coast of Quadra Island. The main attraction of this location is the sunken wreck of an old BC ferry. The story goes that, although deliberately sunk to make an artificial reef, it was originally intended for a deeper site. Its actual resting place is in a mere 10 metres of water, making this a perfect wreck dive for snorkellers. Indeed, at tides below about 2 metres you'll be able to see the rusty carcass breaking the surface.

The wreck is home to large numbers of giant plumose anemones; along with the abundant urchin population, these will dominate your underwater viewing. At the northern end of the wreck, there are also a few crimson anemones, and the short plumose variety is here in force too. On the western side of the hull, a section of black and white tiling conjures a whimsical image of underwater chess, where the urchins take on plumose anemones in a grandmaster game. If you follow the chess set away from the wreck (due west), you can find some small orange sea pens growing on the sandy bottom.

The fun of exploring the wreck, along with the chance of spotting several rarer critters (crimson anemones, Puget Sound king crab, orange sea pens), makes this a memorable North Island destination.

Move the urchin to checkmate—underwater chess on the deck of a wrecked BC ferry.

Signature species

Giant plumose anemones and urchins abound. The wreck is also covered with delicate orange cup corals.

Critter list

Short plumose anemone, giant plumose anemone, crimson anemone, ochre star, leather star, mottled star, blood star, armpit blood star, sunflower star, rainbow star, orange sea cucumber, armoured sea cucumber, giant California sea cucumber, green urchin, red urchin, lined chiton, giant Pacific chiton, kelp greenling, northern abalone, noble sea lemon, orange sea pen, Puget Sound king crab, orange cup coral.

Access

May Island is located about 8 kilometres north of Campbell River. Access to the island (and the wreck) is only by boat. The closest Campbell River launch option is at Discovery Marina; for a free alternative, there is the Big Rock boat ramp to the south of town. The water around the wreck is not deep (about 10 metres), so it is possible to drop anchor here (please don't tie-off on the wreck itself, which risks damaging the structure and the critters living on it). However, given the active current, a live boat is definitely preferable. There are several companies in Campbell River with whom you can organize a charter. The wreck is just off the northern tip of May Island; even at high tide, you should be able to see it from the surface (unless the visibility is atrocious!). Coordinates (in decimal degrees) are: 50.091311, −125.258153.

Tips

If booking a charter, you may be able to get a discount for being a snorkeller (no tanks required). As with all Discovery Passage locations, the current here can be fierce and unpredictable.

45 ROW AND BE DAMNED COVE (Quadra Island)

Famed for its walls of strawberry anemones, Row and Be Damned is one of Discovery Passage's premier scuba diving locations. Although this scuba crowd-pleaser is too deep for us snorkellers, in the cove just to the south of the main site you can glimpse small patches of strawberry anemones in the shallows.

The shoreline of the cove is made of small boulders, a terrain that continues underwater with a fairly steep drop-off. In the springtime, hundreds of orange sea cucumbers emerge to feed, lighting up the sea floor with splashes of colour. The boulders themselves are speckled with orange cup corals, which add to the oceanic colour scheme. The delicate strawberry anemones, whose individuals are no more than a centimetre across, can be found in small clusters on boulder overhangs. Apart from these gems, the wildlife offerings here are rather limited, but the chance to see the underwater strawberries in such shallow water is definitely deserving of a visit.

Signature species
Strawberry anemones, orange cup corals and orange sea cucumbers.

Critter list
Ochre star, leather star, mottled star, orange cup coral, strawberry anemone, Nanaimo dorid, red urchin, purple urchin, orange sea

cucumber, stiff-footed sea cucumber, kelp greenling, copper rockfish, northern abalone, giant rock scallop.

Strawberry anemones.

Access

There is no public beach access along this part of Quadra's coastline, so you need to approach by boat. The closest launch option is Quathiaski Cove, about a kilometre away. In theory, this is easily close enough for kayak access. However, the very strong currents in Discovery Passage mean that you would have to expertly time your arrival, snorkel and return to make this a feasible option. Indeed, the name of this location hints at the perils of a poorly timed paddle. Instead, it is strongly advised to rely on a motor, launched from either Quathiaski Cove or Campbell River. There is a convenient beach for you to land on and then snorkel from the shore. Coordinates (in decimal degrees) are: 50.051743, −125.229099.

Tips

As with all locations along Discovery Passage, the currents can be very strong here.

46

PLUMPER WALL

The Plumper Islands (or Plumper Group) are located just off the northwest coast of Hanson Island and are named after HMS *Plumper*, which surveyed BC's coastline in the mid-19th century. There are several world-class dive sites in this area, thanks to the steep underwater topography and the nutriment-bearing current that rips through Weynton Passage to the southwest. Plumper Wall is one such spot, located near the northern tip of the main central island of the archipelago. As the name suggests, the rock face drops off steeply, but with enough gradient and small shelves for a beautiful kelp forest to take root, home to impressive numbers of fish.

In terms of the invertebrate life, Plumper Wall has two distinct sections. First is the west-facing wall (south from the point), which is covered in small white and peach-coloured plumose anemones, a scaled-down version of Browning Wall (see entry below). There are also clumps of red soft coral (a North Island specialty) and several other anemone species, including a few crimsons and bucketloads of brooding anemones. The net result is an Impressionist canvas in a pastel palette, with the added bonus of the fish-rich kelp forest populated with sizable schools of black and copper rockfish, as well as numerous smaller species. Heading north along the wall and following the coast around to the east is just a matter of a few dozen metres. Although the topography remains steep, being out of the current of the channel means the anemones are now absent, but replaced by plentiful sea star species.

Signature species

Basket stars (which are technically brittle stars) are a real treat for divers and snorkellers alike. Normally found only in the moderate-to-deep subtidal zone, basket stars are a very rare sight for snorkellers, and yet they are plentiful at Plumper Wall at depths of only about 5 metres.

In addition to the commonly found plumose anemones, the much rarer crimson anemones are also plentiful, as are the dainty striped brooding anemones, with their clusters of young.

Critter list

Short plumose anemone, giant plumose anemone, spotted pink anemone, brooding anemone, painted anemone, crimson anemone, kelp greenling, lingcod, black rockfish, copper rockfish, armoured sea cucumber, blood star, leather star, striped sunstar, basket star, mottled star, red urchin, green urchin, giant rock scallop, black leather chiton, lined chiton, giant Pacific chiton, yellow margin dorid, red soft coral, orange cup coral, orange zoanthid, yellow sponge, northern feather duster worm, calcareous tube worm, cross jelly, lion's mane jelly.

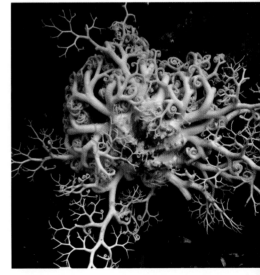

Access

The shoreline of this dive is along the Ksui-La-Das Reserve. The closest boat approach is from Telegraph Cove. Coordinates (in decimal degrees) are: 50.592161, −126.797919.

The water is sufficiently deep here that anchoring is

Basket star.

not an option. If you want to leave your boat unattended, you'll need to find a crevice in the steep rocky shore to wedge your anchor into (not easy), or tie-off on the kelp. If you do anchor on the shore, be aware that the invertebrate life inhabits the rock all the way to the surface, so take care not to damage any animals. By far the best option is to come with a live boat—your buddies will have plenty to occupy them while they bob on the surface, as sea lions and birdlife are plentiful. I have even seen humpback whales just north of the passage, lunge feeding through bait balls (another reason for snorkellers to stick close to the wall!).

Tips

When planning your visit to Plumper Wall, looking at the current chart (for Weynton Passage) is more important than timing with the tide height. There are anemones all the way up the wall, so timing with the very lowest tide is not critical, but you do need to make sure that the current is not ripping. There can be several hours' difference between "slack current" and "low tide" in this area.

Since this snorkel makes a curve around the coastline, you have some flexibility when it comes to finding protected water (i.e., out of wind or current). Even if the current is pulling moderately hard in Weynton Passage on an ebb tide, the more northeasterly part of the route will be protected.

There is significant boat traffic in this area, including the large whale watching boats that depart Telegraph Cove regularly throughout the summer months.

⭐ KULDEKDUMA CHANNEL (Pearse Islands)

47

Located in the Queen Charlotte Strait, at the western end of the Johnstone Strait, the Pearse Islands lie midway between Cormorant Island (home of Alert Bay) and Hanson Island. Several of the Pearse Islands are within Cormorant Channel Marine Provincial Park (along with islands in the Plumper Group, to the east). With its network of channels, hidden beaches and kelp-forested shallows, the Pearse archipelago is one of my favourite island groups to explore by boat. Add in the abundant bird life (bald eagles, kingfishers and shearwaters, to name a few), the seals sunbathing on the tide-exposed rocks, and a major humpback whale highway to the north, and you have another top-notch North Island location.

For the snorkeller, the current-fed channels through the Pearse Islands offer a myriad of opportunities. Kuldekduma Channel is one such spot; because it's no more than about 10 metres deep, on a typical late-summer or fall day the visibility will likely be good enough that you can see all the way to the rock/sand bottom. The base of the channel is mostly covered by large red urchins, happily munching their way through the kelp that is anchored in the shallows. You'll also find orange sea cucumbers and striped sunstars along the bottom.

However, most of the interesting stuff is along the channel walls. Like many of the current-ripped locales in the North Island, much of the rock wall on either side of the channel is richly covered with short and giant plumose anemones, reaching all the way to the sea floor. Most of the plumose anemones here are

Northern abalone.

white, but there are several clumps of the orange colour variety on the Kuldekduma Island side of the channel that are particularly lovely. There is also a decent range of sea stars here (I counted half a dozen species), though by number they are soundly dominated by the mottled variety in its numerous colour morphs.

Signature species

Plumose anemones... everywhere.

Critter list

Short plumose anemone, giant plumose anemone, painted anemone, brooding anemone, striped sunstar, ochre star, mottled star, leather star, blood star, rainbow star, orange sea cucumber, black sea cucumber, giant California sea cucumber, calcareous tube worm, northern abalone, giant rock scallop, black leather chiton, lined chiton, green urchin, red urchin, orange cup coral.

Access

It's a straight shot of about 3 kilometres from Telegraph Cove across the Johnstone Strait to the northeastern tip of the Pearse Islands, or a few kilometres longer if approaching from Alert Bay. The narrow, 200-metre-long Kuldekduma Channel runs between Kuldekduma Island and the island at the northeasterly point of the Pearse Group. Coordinates (in decimal degrees) are: 50.587502, −126.837927.

There are no obvious places to beach a kayak (and Kuldekduma Island is a First Nations Reserve), but there are several lower bank sections on both sides of the channel where you can tie-off your boat around rocks. Alternatively, you could drop anchor in the channel itself, although ideally you should send one of your party down to take a look for wildlife below before you drop it over the side (worry not if you happen to take out an urchin or two—the kelp will thank you for it).

Tips

The current can run fairly quickly through the channel; it is preferable to snorkel here at ebb tide, when things move more slowly, but the water here seems always to be on the move.

While you're out this way, combine this location with Northeast Pearse (see the next entry), just around the corner. In particular, if you have struggled to enjoy the deeper terrain of Northeast Pearse, Kuldekduma offers easier depths, and on a good visibility day, you won't need to dive at all to enjoy the anemone show.

TUBE WORMS

Tube worms appear like tiny, colourful starbursts in the intertidal zone. Because they are often found in the shallows, requiring no diving, you can linger at your leisure and be hypnotized by the gentle waft of their feathery tentacles. But don't get too close—many species of tube worms have numerous compound eyes around their feathery crowns and will quickly retract if you get too close.

NORTHEAST PEARSE ISLAND

48

Just around the corner from Kuldekduma Channel is another of the area's premier scuba dive sites. The petite, 200-metre-long, northeasterly member of the Pearse Islands is particularly famed for its plumose anemone–coated wall. Unlike some of the other "wall" locations in this section (such as Browning or Plumper), the wall here does not drop off immediately from the waterline. Instead, the terrain descends via a couple of shelves that extend about 20 metres offshore. These shelves, which bottom out around 7–10 metres down, are marked by profuse kelp growth in the summertime. Beyond the kelp line is where the wall drops down vertically.

If you stay on the inside of the kelp growth, you will enjoy some modest anemone and sea star offerings. But farther offshore is where the action really starts. The kelp forest is rich in fish, most notably large groups of black rockfish. Once clear of the kelp, on a good visibility day, you'll be able to see down to the deeper shelf. Diving down to take a closer look, you'll be able to make out abundant short white plumose that carpet the bottom, with a few red soft corals and yellow sponges. I even spotted a basket star—a rare sight for snorkellers (go to Plumper Wall for the best chance to spot these beautiful brittle beasties). Competent freedivers will be able to take a look over the edge of the wall, which starts at 7–10 metres. This vertical section is nothing short of a plumose avalanche—a pure, dense, white curtain descending into the abyss.

The spotted pink (top) and crimson (bottom) anemones have a similar candy-floss colour, with white polka dots on their trunks. However, the crimson anemone has delicate pale bandings on its tentacles.

Signature species

Short plumose anemones on the deeper shelves and in incredible density on the wall.

Critter list

Short plumose anemone, giant plumose anemone, painted anemone, green surf anemone, spotted pink anemone, brooding anemone, crimson anemone, orange sea cucumber, striped sunstar, ochre star, mottled star, leather star, basket star, green urchin, giant Pacific chiton, black leather chiton, black rockfish, kelp greenling, red soft coral, yellow sponge.

Access

The approach to Northeast Pearse is the same as to Kuldekduma Channel—shortest from Telegraph Cove or Alert Bay. There is a convenient notch in the coastline at the northern point of the east-facing coast in which you can park a small boat out of any current. The bottom here is shallow enough to either drop an anchor or tie-off on the shoreline. This is also a convenient location to disembark and gear up on dry land. Coordinates (in decimal degrees) are: 50.587652, −126.833560.

Tips

The current here is fierce—use the kelp status to help you judge whether the conditions are manageable and always err on the side of caution. Snorkel this location on an ebb tide (according to the Weynton Passage current tables) in order to be at least partly sheltered from the current.

Given the depths of the most interesting terrain, this is a site best appreciated by snorkellers with some freediving ability. However, Northeast Pearse pairs well with Kuldekduma Channel, which offers lots of anemones at shallower depths.

49 MASTERMAN ISLANDS

Located at the mouth of Hardy Bay, about 5 kilometres from the town of Port Hardy, the Masterman Islands are named after Sir Thomas Masterman Hardy, erstwhile vice admiral of the British Royal Navy. Spread out over about a kilometre, the archipelago consists of around a dozen individual islands. The two principal islands sandwich a handful of smaller islets between them, forming a shallow, sheltered central area. The soft, sandy bottom here is ideal for burrowing molluscs, and plentiful moon snail egg coils can be seen in the shallows. The shallow depth and protected aspect make for an ideal anchorage. In the summertime, these islets host rich kelp beds, and seals use the low-lying waterfront as a haul-out. You will surely have some of these curious critters come and check you out! A small south-facing notch in the largest of the islands hosts a fine sand/shell beach that is ideal for kayak landings. Roughly half a dozen islets scattered to the west complete the archipelago.

Viewed from the surface, the shoreline looks as if it will plunge vertically, which indeed it does, but not very deep. At low tide, the vertical rock descends only about 5 metres or so, before levelling out to a sandy shingle bottom that then slopes away gently from the shore. For the snorkeller, this is perfect terrain, as these short rock walls are packed with critters that don't take much diving to appreciate. Curiously, I did not see a single nudibranch, or many fish, but sea stars and anemones were here in abundance—every parting of the kelp revealed some colourful splash at eye level.

Painted anemones can be found in a variety of colours—most commonly green and red, but sometimes also pink and white.

Signature species

There are numerous colonies of plumose on the vertical rock walls just a few metres below the surface. Luminous green surf anemones populate the cracks and crevices of the west shore, and variously coloured painted anemones abound to boot. Large ochre stars are also here in abundance, in both bright purple and orange, as well as numerous other sea star species.

Critter list

Ochre star, leather star, mottled star, blood star, rose star, sunflower star, rainbow star, vermilion star, green surf anemone, pink-tipped aggregating anemone, painted anemone, short plumose anemone, giant plumose anemone, white-spotted rose anemone, shiny sea squirt, northern staghorn bryozoan, orange sea cucumber, giant California sea cucumber, purple urchin, red urchin, moon snail, great sculpin.

Access

The Masterman Islands are about 5 kilometres from Port Hardy, a distance that is either eminently kayakable or a brief sprint under horsepower. The most convenient put-in for boats and kayaks is at Bear Cove, located on the opposite shore from Port Hardy, about a 10-minute drive from downtown and just before the BC Ferries terminal. The boat ramp here is excellent; it is wide and well maintained, has no launching or parking charges, and comes equipped with a hose for a post-excursion spray-down (of your boat, not you).

Cruise north out of Hardy Bay; the Masterman Islands are located just a few hundred metres off the northern tip of the peninsula. The main cluster of islands offers a protected anchorage, and the small pocket beach on the southern shore of the largest island provides a good spot to land a kayak.

Tips

I was fortunate to visit the Masterman Islands on a calm day, and I experienced zero current. However, the profusion of current- and surf-loving species, such as the green anemones, hints that such benign conditions are not the norm. The prevailing weather pattern here is for northwest winds to blow in after noon, so check conditions before you head out, particularly if you plan to linger into the post-meridiem.

BROWNING WALL
(Nigei Island)

50

Browning Wall will take your breath away the moment you put your face in the water. The scale of the vertical cliff and the overwhelming profusion of intertidal life are nothing short of magnificent, and no amount of superlative prose can prepare you for the experience. Simply put, Browning Wall is *the* premier snorkelling location around Vancouver Island, and the star rating given here is an underwater understatement. And you don't just have to take my word for it; diving legend Jacques Cousteau rated Browning Wall in his top 10 temperate (as opposed to tropical) dive sites on the planet.

Located adjacent to the wonderfully named God's Pocket Marine Provincial Park, Browning Wall drops off 100 vertical metres from the east coast of Nigei Island, in the channel that faces Balaklava Island. The combination of this vertiginous rock face and the significant currents that get funnelled through Browning Pass generates an underwater utopia for cold-water filter feeders. The lack of any "bottom" (or available real estate on the wall itself) means that vegetation here is minimal year-round.

It is not an exaggeration to say that every inch of the wall is covered in life, from the surface to as far as you'll be able to hold your breath. Although the most obvious species are the white and peach plumose anemones, there are also plentiful surf and painted varieties that extend the palette of pastels to bright greens and reds. The cnidarian canvas is punctuated with bursts of soft red coral and multi-hued compound tunicate colonies, as well as oversized acorn barnacles snatching at the current. All of this colour is topped off by large numbers of bright orange and purple ochre stars, which seem to fight for space in the crevices and upper intertidal zone.

Signature species

White and orange plumose anemones extend from the surface to as far as the eye can see. This plumose wallpaper is dotted with clumps of red soft coral—although these species are present in other local spots (such as Seven Tree Island), the abundance here is stunning, and the backdrop of anemones makes for a beautiful pastel canvas.

Red soft coral.

Critter list

Short plumose anemone, painted anemone, rose anemone, giant plumose anemone, pink-tipped aggregating anemone, green surf anemone, opalescent nudibranch, ochre star, mottled star, blood star, giant acorn barnacle, calcareous tube worm, northern feather duster worm, yellow sponge, red soft coral, purple urchin, orange sea cucumber, stiff-footed sea cucumber, lined chiton, black leather chiton, stalked compound tunicate, mushroom compound tunicate.

Access

Browning Wall is about 20 kilometres from Port Hardy. Upon exiting Hardy Bay, pass Duval Point heading west, cross Goletas Channel and enter Browning Pass between Nigei and Balaklava islands. Hussar Point is at the southern tip of a spur on the east side of Nigei, and the wall starts just north of this. Coordinates (in decimal degrees) are: 50.847794, −127.64476.

There is nowhere to land a boat or kayak, no possibility to anchor owing to the deep water, and no kelp to tie-off onto. As a result, you will need a live boat to snorkel at Browning Wall. While it is certainly possible to do this under your own steam, either as a day trip under horsepower out of Port Hardy or as part of a kayak tour from God's Pocket, be aware that wind and water conditions here can turn on a dime—a calm morning can blow into a significant gale in the afternoon, and strong currents can rip through Goletas Channel. It is therefore recommended to throw some money at the situation and book a charter.

Tips

The legendary visibility here usually starts in early September. However, dive charters typically only run until the end of October, after which the weather gets too gnarly. This narrow seasonal window means that dive charters are usually booked for September/October dates a year in advance. However, for snorkellers, late August is just as good, and tours can often be booked with much shorter notice.

51 SEVEN TREE ISLAND (off Nigei Island)

Located about halfway up Browning Pass, Seven Tree is a modest islet a few tens of metres offshore from Nigei Island. Although the islet is topped with a small copse, the trees definitely outnumber the advertised seven, so do not be misled and think you have the wrong spot. The west side of Seven Tree drops down a mere

Rainbow star.

10–15 metres toward Nigei, levelling out to a sandy shingle bottom that boasts a handsome collection of orange sea pens. The shallow depths are also an ideal kelp forest habitat, and you will find plenty of critters among the fronds, including numerous snail species and brooding anemones.

The east side of the island descends to much greater depths, and hosts much of the same current-loving wildlife as Browning Wall, albeit in more modest proportions. Plumose anemones abound, and you'll also find clumps of red soft coral and the usual tunicate menagerie. This is a delightful spot to

Brooding anemones exhibit striped trunks and disks, and often have offspring clustered around their base.

circumnavigate, current permitting, and one that is easily combined with Browning Wall.

Signature species

Orange sea pens are fairly plentiful along the shingle bottom on the west side of the island. I also greatly enjoyed the abundance of brooding anemones inhabiting the kelp fronds, including some in a particularly lovely blue colour.

Critter list

Green surf anemone, short plumose anemone, white-spotted rose anemone, brooding anemone, painted anemone, crimson anemone, red soft coral, mushroom compound tunicate, purple urchin, orange sea pen, blood star, ochre star, mottled star, rainbow star, colourful six-armed star, leather star, kelp greenling, painted greenling, orange sea cucumber, giant rock scallop.

Access

As with many of the dive sites in this area, the name Seven Tree Island is an unofficial moniker that has developed in the local vernacular, but not one you will find on any map or with the aid of Google! Coordinates (in decimal degrees) are: 50.861326, −127.654748. There is no beach to land on, so if coming in your own craft, you will likely have to either tie-off on some kelp or find a shallow spot on the west side to drop anchor (but send a snorkeller down first to check out the terrain—you don't want to drop it on a sea pen!). However, your best bet is coming by charter, which will allow you to combine Browning Wall, Seven Tree Island and several other sites on a single outing.

Tips

Access to the orange sea pens requires a dive of at least 10 metres, so timing with low tide is important.

Diamondback tritonia.

Pacific sea peach.

ACKNOWLEDGEMENTS

My goal in writing this guide was to pass on my knowledge of how and where to snorkel around Vancouver Island. Although some of this wisdom has been accrued through personal trial and error, this would have been an immeasurably longer and more painful process were it not for expert input from other seasoned snorkellers and divers. For everything from tips on the warmest wetsuits and intel on top destinations, to expert species identification and advice on all things camera-related, I am indebted to Karolle Wall, Mark Cantwell, Mark Hiebert and Brian Chapel.

Snorkelling requires buddies, and I have some of the best! Thanks to Nathan and Felysia Green, Maureen Scott, Kim Venn, Adam Ritz, Natasha and Henry Parsons, and Alima Ali. I am grateful for all our adventures and discoveries, and hope that we will enjoy many more together (after all, we now have to start research for the second edition...).

For invaluable advice and guidance in navigating the world of publishing, thanks to Andy Lamb, Rick Harbo and Theo Dombrowski. A heartfelt thanks to the superlative staff at Harbour for their belief in the project and in particular to Becky Pruitt MacKenney and Emma Biron who made the production process a breeze. J. Duane Sept generously lent his professional expertise by both reading a draft manuscript and producing the species appendix.

Steve and Trudy Lacasse of Sun Fun Divers generously shared their expert knowledge of North Island dive spots and took us on an unforgettable trip to Browning Wall. Roger McDonell and Greg Baldock from Oceanfix.ca Dive Centre in Campbell River showed us a great time in Discovery Passage—with bonus orcas! During the research and writing of the North Island chapter, my family was the fortunate beneficiary of the warmth and hospitality of TerryLynn Gold and Colin Ritchie at the Seine Boat Inn in Alert Bay; we arrived as guests and left as friends.

But my biggest words of gratitude go to my patient and long-suffering husband, and the captain of my boat, Jon. Thank you for enduring my continual snorkel-lust and occasional grumpiness when things don't go according to plan, and for waiting in the boat (in the rain) when I don't want to come back in. This book would quite simply not have happened without your (mostly) gentle persuasion to turn my passion into pages.

Oval anchored stalked jelly.

SPECIES LIST
(Alphabetical by Phylum)

Arthropods

acorn barnacle, *Balanus glandula*
giant acorn barnacle, *Balanus glandula*
gooseneck barnacle,
    Pollicipes polymorphus
heart crab, *Phyllolithodes papillosus*
northern kelp crab, *Pugettia producta*
Puget Sound king crab,
    Lopholithodes mandtii
red rock crab, *Cancer productus*
sharpnose crab, *Scyra acutifrons*
umbrella crab, *Cryptolithodes sitchensis*

Sea Anemones, Jellies & Comb Jellies

brooding anemone, *Epiactis lisbethae*
comb jelly, *Pleurobrachia bachei*
crimson anemone, *Cribrinopsis rubens*
cross jelly, *Mitrocoma cellularia*
crystal jelly, *Aequorea victoria*
fried egg jelly,
    Phacellophora camtschatica
giant plumose anemone,
    Metridium farcimen
green surf anemone,
    Anthopleura xanthogrammica
lion's mane jelly, *Cyanea capillata*
moon jelly, *Aurelia labiata*
red-eyed medusa, *Polyorchis penicillatus*

moonglow anemone,
    Anthopleura artemisia
orange cup coral, *Balanophyllia elegans*
orange sea pen, *Ptilosarcus gurneyi*
orange zoanthid, *Epizoanthus scotinus*
oval anchored stalked jelly,
    Haliclystus stejnegeri
painted anemone, *Urticina grebelnyi*
pink-tipped aggregating anemone,
    Anthopleura elegantissima
red soft coral, *Gersemia rubiformis*
rose anemone, *Urticina piscivora*
short plumose anemone,
    Metridium senile
strawberry anemone,
    Corynactis californica
stubby rose anemone, *Urticina coriacea*
spotted pink anemone,
    Aulactinia vancouverensis
tube-dwelling anemone,
    Pachycerianthus fimbriatus
white-spotted rose anemone,
    Cribrinopsis albopunctata

Molluscs

Aleutian moon snail,
    Cryptonatica aleutica
California mussel, *Mytilus californianus*
black leather chiton, *Katharina tunicata*
branched dendronotid,
    Dendronotus venustus

giant Pacific chiton, *Cryptochiton stelleri*
gaper clam, *Tresus* sp.
giant Pacific octopus,
     Enteroctopus dofleini
giant rock scallop, *Crassadoma gigantea*
clown nudibranch, *Triopha* sp.
Cockerell's dorid, *Limacia cockerelli*
diamondback tritonia, *Tritonia festiva*
frosted nudibranch, *Dirona albolineata*
giant white dorid, *Doris odhneri*
golden dirona, *Dirona pellucida*
giant dendronotid, *Dendronotus iris*
Heath's dorid, *Geitodoris heathi*
hooded nudibranch, *Melibe leonina*
Hudson's dorid, *Acanthodoris hudsoni*
leopard nudibranch (leopard dorid),
     Diaulula odonoghuei
Lewis's moon snail, *Euspira lewisii*
lined chiton, *Tonicella lineata*
modest cadlina, *Triopha modesta*
Monterey dorid (Monterey
     nudibranch), *Doris montereyensis*
mossy chiton, *Mopalia muscosa*
multicolour dendronotid,
     Dendronotus albus
Nanaimo dorid,
     Acanthodoris nanaimoensis
noble sea lemon, *Peltodoris nobilis*
northern abalone,
     Haliotis kamtschatkana
opalescent (long-horned) nudibranch,
     Hermissenda crassicornis
orange peel nudibranch,
     Tochuina tetraquetra
pink scallop, *Chlamys* sp.
red sponge dorid, *Rostanga pulchra*
red-gilled nudibranch,
     Flabellina verrucosa
red Pacific octopus, *Octopus rubescens*
San Diego dorid, *Diaulula sandiegensis*
shag-rug (shaggy mouse) nudibranch,
     Aeolidia papillosa
three-lined aeolid, *Orienthella trilineata*
white berthella, *Berthella chacei*

white-and-orange-tipped nudibranch,
     Janolus fuscus
winged sea slug, *Gastropteron pacificum*
yellow margin dorid,
     Cadlina luteomarginata

Echinoderms

armoured sea cucumber,
     Psolus chitonoides
armpit blood star, *Henricia* sp. A
bat star, *Patiria miniata*
basket star, *Gorgonocephalus eucnemis*
black sea cucumber, *Pseudocnus curatus*
blood star, *Henricia leviuscula*
colourful six-armed star,
     Leptasterias aequalis
cushion (slime) star, *Pteraster tesselatus*
drab six-armed star,
     Leptasterias hexactis
giant California sea cucumber,
     Apostichopus californicus
giant pink star, *Pisaster brevispinus*
green urchin,
     Strongylocentrotus droebachiensis
leather star, *Dermasterias imbricata*
mottled star, *Evasterias troschelii*
northern sunstar, *Solaster endeca*
ochre star, *Pisaster ochraceus*
orange sea cucumber,
     Cucumaria miniata
pale sea cucumber, *Cucumaria pallida*
purple urchin,
     Strongylocentrotus purpuratus
rainbow star, *Orthasterias koehleri*
red urchin, *Mesocentrotus franciscanus*
rose star, *Crossaster papposus*
spiny red star, *Hippasteria spinosa*
stiff-footed sea cucumber,
     Eupentacta quinquesemita
striped sunstar, *Solaster stimpsoni*
sunflower star, *Pycnopodia helianthoides*
velcro star, *Stylasterias forreri*
vermilion star, *Mediaster aequalis*

Misc. Invertebrates

calcareous tube worm,
Serpula columbiana
hermit crab sponge,
Suberites domuncula latus
northern feather duster worm,
Eudistylia vancouveri
northern staghorn bryozoan,
Heteropora pacifica
polymorph feather duster worm,
Eudistylia polymorpha
slime tube feather duster worm,
Myxicola infundibulum

Tunicates

lightbulb tunicate, *Clavelina huntsmani*
lined compound tunicate,
Botrylloides violaceus
lobed compound tunicate,
Cystodytes lobatus
mauve lobed tunicate,
Eudistoma purpuropunctatum
mushroom compound tunicate,
Distaplia occidentalis
orange social tunicate,
Metandrocarpa taylori
Pacific sea peach,
Halocynthia aurantium
shiny sea squirt,
Cnemidocarpa finmarkiensis
stalked compound tunicate,
Distaplia smithi

Fish

bay pipefish, *Sygnathus leptorhynchusb*
blackeye goby, *Rhinogobiops nicholsii*
black rockfish, *Sebastes melanops*
buffalo sculpin, *Enophrys bison*
cabezon, *Scorpaenichthys marmoratus*
copper rockfish, *Sebastes caurinus*
crescent gunnel, *Pholis laeta*
great sculpin, *Myoxocephalus*
polyacanthocephalus
kelp greenling, *Hexagrammos*
decagrammus
lingcod, *Ophiodon elongatus*
northern clingfish,
Gobiesox maeandricus
Pacific herring, *Clupea pallasii*
painted greenling, *Oxylebius pictus*
penpoint gunnel, *Apodichthys flavidus*
pile perch, *Rhacochilus vacca*
rock greenling,
Hexagrammos lagocephalus
shiner perch, *Cymatogaster aggregata*
smoothhead sculpin, *Artedius lateralis*
Pacific spiny lumpsucker,
Eumicrotremus orbis
sixgill shark, *Hexanchus griseus*
wolf-eel, *Anarrhichthys ocellatus*

Seaweeds (Algae)

bull kelp, *Nereocystis luetkeana*
dead man's fingers,
Halosaccion glandiforme
feather boa kelp, *Egregia menziesii*
giant kelp, *Macrocystis pyrifera*
rockweed, *Fucus* sp.

INDEX

Note: Page numbers in **bold** refer to photographs or illustrations

ABOUT THE AUTHOR

Sara Ellison is a professional astrophysicist and a significant leader in the field of galaxy evolution. She is also an avid sportswoman, triathlete and world traveller. She lives in Victoria, BC.

Photo by Jon Willis